complete
ceramics

complete ceramics

EASY TECHNIQUES AND OVER 20 GREAT PROJECTS

COLLINS & BROWN

First published in the United Kingdom in 2009 by
Collins & Brown
10 Southcombe Street
London
W14 0RA

An imprint of Anova Books Company Ltd

Distributed in the United States and Canada by
Sterling Publishing Co, 387 Park Avenue South,
New York, NY 10016-8810, USA

ISBN 978-1-84340-482-8

A CIP catalogue for this book is available from the
British Library.

10 9 8 7 6 5 4 3 2 1

Reproduction by Rival Colour Ltd, UK
Printed and bound by SNP Leefung, China

This book can be ordered direct from the publisher.
Contact the marketing department, but try your
bookshop first.

www.anovabooks.com

contents

history

The making of pottery is an ancient art – as early as 29,000–25,000BCE figurines were made from clay and fired in bonfires or kilns partially dug into the ground. The earliest known pottery vessels are believed to date from the Jomon period (about 10,500–400BCE) in Japan, and show a unique sophistication of technique and design. The first use of functional pottery to store water and food is thought to have been around 9,000 or 10,000BCE, when the development of agriculture led to a need to store produce. Pots were fired but not glazed – although examples dating back to 6,000BCE that are burnished to make them watertight have been found in some parts of Europe. However, it was the invention of the potter's wheel in Mesopotamia in the Ubaid period (between 6,000 and 4,000BCE) that revolutionized the production of pottery.

Decorative arts

The exact origin of glazes and glazing techniques is unknown, but the fine lustrous glazes developed in China probably began with a simple glaze to make earthenware watertight. Chinese potters came to regard glazes as being of great importance; in the Han period (100–200) they used lead glaze with wood ash added to create a mottled dull brown or grey-green colour that was occasionally iridescent. Coloured glazes were developed and used by T'ang (618–907) and Song (960–1279) dynasty potters, and a wide range of brightly coloured ceramics soon began to appear. Pure white porcelain, or blanc de Chine, first appeared during the Ming dynasty (1368–1644) and Te-hua potters in Fukien province soon produced blanc de Chine masterpieces in the purest white porcelain coated with a thick white glaze.

Decorative brush painting on ceramics reached its height in China during the Ming dynasty. In the 13th century ceramics from Persia painted in blue cobalt under the glaze inspired the Chinese blue-and-white style, but Ming artists also excelled in painting over the glaze in brilliant enamel colours. Overglaze enamel decorations from the Chenghua period (1465–87) incorporated flowers, foliage and figures against backgrounds of arabesques and scrollwork.

In Japan glazed wares were produced from an early date, but Japanese glazed stoneware really developed after warlord Toyotomi Hideyoshi's abortive invasions of Korea – the so-called 'Potters Wars' – in 1594 and 1597. Although military failures, the wars led to Korean potters being brought to Japan to start new potteries or revitalize flagging Japanese kilns. Soon the rough yet refined Raku stoneware was developed, as well as the superb enamel decoration of the Edo period (1615–1868).

In Greece the potter's art developed from around 10,000BCE through the Minoan (2700–1450BCE) and Mycenaean (1600–1100BCE) civilizations, culminating from the 6th–4th centuries BCE in a unique type of painted pottery. Attic vases are exquisitely proportioned and often decorated with finely painted relief work. The unique gloss on such vases – and similar wares made elsewhere in Greece at the same time – is not a glaze or a varnish, and is more marked in the areas painted black. It was achieved by applying layers of special slip then firing in a carbonaceous atmosphere.

Developments in the West

After the fall of the Roman Empire in 476, potters in Europe produced mainly utilitarian items until the end of the Middle Ages in the 16th century. An exception was a distinctive type of earthenware known as majolica, which was derived from Chinese porcelain and appeared in Italy during the last quarter of the 14th century. It was inspired by Spanish lusterware introduced to Italy by Majorcan seagoing traders. Majolica ware could be thrown on the wheel or press moulded, fired once to a brown or buff body, then dipped in opaque glaze to achieve a surface suitable for decoration. A second firing after decoration fixed the white glaze to the body and the pigments to the glaze, so colours became permanent. The work of Luca della Robbia (1400–82) raised majolica production from a craft to high art in Italy.

In the early 1700s English potters often used salt glaze, but also produced a slip-decorated earthenware that was a speciality of the Toft family. Delftware, a kind of tin-glazed earthenware produced in the Netherlands, was among the first European pottery to be decorated with motifs inspired by Chinese and Japanese styles. European potters tried to imitate porcelain, but the formula remained elusive until ceramist Johann Bottger (1682–1719) discovered its secret. The first European royal porcelain factory was established at Meissen near Dresden, in Germany, but the porcelain formula leaked out and rival factories soon appeared across Europe. The famous Meissen porcelain figures were first produced as part of sweetmeat dishes. In the late 1700s the royal Sevres factory in France was the leading European porcelain factory, perhaps because of the patronage of Madame de Pompadour, Louis XV's mistress. Sevres wares were painted in colours that no other European factory could duplicate, but bleu de roi and rose Pompadour inspired English potters to greater heights.

One of the most enterprising English potters of the late 18th century was Josiah Wedgwood (1730–95). He developed Queen's Ware – a much-improved cream earthenware – his celebrated jasperware and black basalt, and a series of fine figures created by famous artists. In the early 19th century Parian ware was outstandingly popular. A creamy colour, like marble, it was made by several factories, each of which sold it under a different name. Its generic name was coined by Minton after Paros, the Greek island that was the source of an ivory-tinted marble used for sculptures in ancient times. Other English and American potters either obtained details of the original formula or worked out their own, so the production of Parian wares on both sides of the Atlantic was enormous.

Another beautiful and successful ceramic tradition from the 19th century is pâte-sur-pâte, a paste-on-paste technique devised sometime after 1870 by Marc-Louis Solon (1835–1913) at Minton. Pâte-sur-pâte was stained Parian ware decorated with reliefs in translucent tinted or white slip. Solon was inspired by a Chinese celadon case decorated with embossed flowers in the museum at Sevres, where he had worked for a time. Minton wares decorated with pâte-sur-pâte soon became costly and coveted ceramic ornaments produced.

By the late 19th century the age of mass production had dawned and the potter's art suffered until the 20th century. However, in the 1930s signs of revival appeared, due to the work of artist-potters in Western Europe and the United States. Some experimented with materials and techniques, others sought inspiration from pottery traditions around the world, and after the end of the Second World War artist-artisans influenced the design and decoration of commercial ceramics. Individual items that are made by hand are now increasingly valued over mass-produced items, and the craft of ceramics is enjoying an excellent period in its history.

materials & equipment

Clay

Clay is a natural material that has been formed over millions of years from the decomposition of granite or feldspar rocks. In its raw state clay is not usually very pliable or plastic, so other materials are added to make it more workable.

Earthenware clay – This is the most widely available clay and is the least expensive. Red earthenware has a high iron content, giving it a rich terracotta colour when fired. White earthenware is grey before firing and creamy white afterwards, so is more suitable if you want to use coloured glazes. Earthenware clay is fired at quite a low temperature and does not vitrify, so it will remain porous and must be glazed if it is to contain liquids.

Stoneware clay – This is a dense and hard clay that is much stronger than earthenware, and is available in a range of colours from white through to brown. It is also available in different textures from fine to quite coarse. It can be fired to a very high temperature, which will cause the clay particles to vitrify thus making it non porous. Items can still be glazed, either for hygiene or to add decoration.

Porcelain clay – Porcelain is the purest and whitest clay available and is not only quite expensive but quite difficult to handle. It may also distort when fired, so it takes practice and patience to achieve good results. However, it can be worked very thin so it is extremely translucent and fired to very high temperatures, which make it hard and impervious to fluids.

Storage

Clay must be stored in tightly sealed containers to keep it moist, although even then it will eventually dry out in time. Do not store the containers anywhere too warm, or where there is a danger of frost. If the clay does become too hard to work, it can be wedged with softer clay to make it more workable. If it has dried out too much to wedge, break it into small pieces, place in a bowl and cover with warm water. Leave until it has broken down into a thick liquid – which is known as slurry – then spread over a plaster bat to dry, turning regularly until the clay is the right consistency to wedge or knead.

Wedging

Wedging mixes different types of clay thoroughly, either two different types or clays of different consistencies. Cut the two types into slices with the cutting wire, then stack the slices in alternate layers. Beat with your hand to compress the layers together. Cut the block you have formed in half with the cutting wire, stack the two halves of the block and beat together again. Repeat until the two clays have merged into each other.

Kneading

This is essential to remove air bubbles and to distribute the water evenly to prepare the clay for working. It is essentially the same process as kneading bread dough

– hold the clay mass between your hands and press downwards and forwards with the heels of your hands. Gather the clay up and roll it back towards you into a rounded mass. Repeat the pushing and rolling process until all the clay is completely smooth and malleable throughout, with an even texture and no air pockets.

Clay ride

Clay colour can change dramatically when it is fired. If this is going to be an issue in your project, ask the supplier to show you fired samples.

If you don't know which clay to choose for your project to get the result that you want, try asking the supplier for recommendations.

Clay shrinks as it dries and when it is fired. Suppliers can often provide shrinkage rates, but you can also fire measured samples to check for yourself.

It is always a good idea to note exactly what you do as you make a project, including firing times and temperatures. There is nothing more irritating than a happy accident giving a wonderful effect that cannot be repeated!

Slip is liquid clay, which is used for slipcasting and can also be coloured and used in many ways to decorate the surface of clay forms.

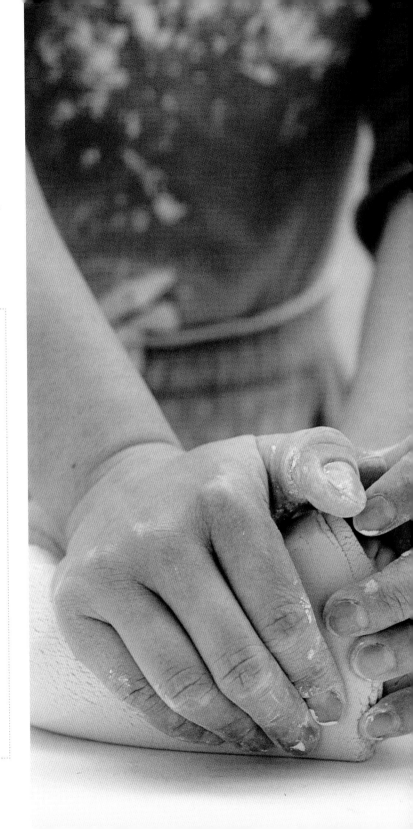

When you start out making your own ceramics you can often manage with only a few tools – many of which could be adapted from ordinary household items. Any special tools that you need can easily be bought from pottery suppliers; there is a selection of good resources listed on pages 157–158.

Basic tools

Cutting wire – Used for cutting pots off a wheel head or bat and when wedging clay.

Potter's needle – For marking lines and for piercing holes.

Hole cutter – The tapered point can be used to make holes of different sizes.

Metal kidney – Available in different sizes and shapes and with a serrated edge and used to work on the clay surface.

Ribbon or loop tools – For trimming and hollowing out shapes, particularly when sculpting clay.

Potter's knife – The serrated edge makes cutting wet clay easier.

Rubber kidney – Ideal for fine smoothing and compacting of the clay surface.

Rasp (surform) blade – A standard tool in most household toolboxes, which can be used in ceramics to pare the clay, level rims or create texture.

Paint scraper – Handy to clean work surfaces before washing down.

Rolling pin – A wooden one without handles is the best type for working on clay. It is used to roll out the clay slab to an even thickness.

Roller guides – For rolling slab, so a selection in various thicknesses is ideal.

Banding wheel or turntable – Useful to rotate an item easily so it can be viewed from all sides as you work.

Wooden modelling tools – Come in many shapes and

Toolbox

There are lots of special tools you can buy for working with clay and plaster, but don't be afraid to use anything from around the house or kitchen that you think will be suitable. For instance, old credit cards are good as scrapers, old butter knives are good for shaping, inexpensive plastic kitchen utensils can be cut down.

Once you have used a kitchen utensil on clay it should never be returned to the kitchen and used for food.

A chuck is a form to hold a pot upside-down above the wheel head while it is trimmed. Chucks are thrown and bisque-fired clay cylinders open on both sides.

sizes, but a small selection can be used in a wide range of ways.

Wooden ribs – Available in many shapes and sizes and used in throwing to smooth and refine the shape.

Wooden spoons and spatulas – Can be sourced from a kitchenware shop and useful for stirring, beating and texturing clay.

Callipers – Used for measuring and comparing sizes when throwing or turning on the lathe.

Pottery wheel – Essential for throwing pots, can be electric or foot powered.

Decorating tools

Brushes – Collect a good selection of brushes for different uses, such as applying slip or glaze, painting in details, brushing joins and sweeping away bits of clay.

Sponges – Used to remove excess water when throwing, final smoothing of surfaces and to apply slip or glaze.

Slip trailer – These come in different sizes and are designed to give a smooth line of slip, but can be used for other purposes as well.

Homemade tools for shaping, texturing and stamping – Many useful tools can be made from ordinary household objects, such as combs, credit cards, plastic kitchen utensils, scrapers.

Kilns

A kiln is probably the most expensive piece of equipment you will need to invest in if you want to work in ceramics seriously. However to start off with you can probably arrange for your work to be fired at a local college or craft centre or you can try out techniques like raku firing (see page 12). Kilns can be electric, gas or wood, but an electric kiln is probably more practical for non-commercial use as they come in many sizes, are simple to use and are clean. There are two main types of kiln – top-loading and front-loading – each with their own benefits and drawbacks.

Top-loading
Tend to be cheaper
Easier to install
Lighter in weight
May not retain heat as well

Front-loading
Thicker walls
retain heat well
Harder wearing
Substantial and heavy
More expensive to buy and install

The four key points to consider when choosing a kiln are:

How big a kiln do you need? How wide are your doorways – will the kiln will go through? How much will you fire at one time? With a small kiln you may have to fire in batches, but smaller kilns are not costly to fire. Larger kilns can take more items, but if you usually fire a small amount they are not cost effective.

Where am I going to put the kiln? Smaller kilns use a domestic power supply; larger ones may need a special supply. Kilns get hot outside, so place away from walls – although a top-loading kiln can be pushed near a wall or under a table when cool. Don't place a kiln in your work area, unless you only fire when you are not there.

What are you intending to make and fire? Consider the finished size of your work and the sort of temperatures you will need to fire to. Different types and sizes of kilns will have different parameters.

How much can you afford? New kilns are usually more expensive than older ones, but they should be more reliable and cheaper to run. They will also come with a guarantee and it may be easier to get spare parts. A secondhand kiln may look like a bargain – but consider whether it may need an expensive overhaul or more intensive ongoing maintenance.

Bisque firing

Bisque or biscuit is the first firing, which hardens the clay ready for any secondary processes. When bisque firing it doesn't matter if the kiln is packed so items touch each other – you can even stack bowls inside one another as long as they are very loose. Make sure when you load the kiln that the weight is evenly distributed around the shelves.

Glaze firing

The glaze firing adds a final protective coat, although this is not essential with some types of clay – or if the item is just decorative and does not need to be non-porous. When glaze firing, items should never touch each other or they will stick together. Coat the kiln shelf with kiln wash, to stop any drips of glaze from sealing the item to the shelf. Make sure you wipe away excess glaze from any surface of your form that might come into contact with the kiln, to avoid the two surfaces fusing together.

Raku firing

This is an ancient method of firing that was traditionally employed for the items used in the Japanese tea ceremony. The kiln is built outside using fire bricks, or there are special raku kilns that are powered with propane gas. The form is bisque-fired, then coated in a glaze that will melt at a relatively low temperature and fired quickly until it melts. Using tongs, the form is removed from the kiln while still red hot and placed in a reduction chamber, which is usually a drum filled with wood shavings, sawdust or straw. The form is then covered with more shavings before the drum is sealing with a lid. When cool the form can be cleaned with a scouring pad to remove carbon marks and reveal the crackled glaze that is typical of the process, which happens as a result of thermal shock and smoke being absorbed through the crazing.

Cracking up

Since the forms are being handled at high temperatures when raku firing, wear protective clothing and keep a bucket of water nearby in case of accidents.

Your reduction chamber needs to be an airtight container that you can fill with sawdust and seal. It will get hot, so make sure it is heatproof and is standing on a heatproof surface. A metal dustbin with a tight-fitting lid is ideal.

Place the reduction chamber near the kiln – which should be outside because of the fumes generated.

The tongs may mark the molten glaze when you lift the pot out of the kiln, but this is part of the charm of raku wear.

health & safety

The main risk to health whilst working in ceramics is from the clay itself. Clay contains crystalline silica, most of which is chemically combined with other materials, but fine dust particles containing free silica can be invisible to the naked eye and could penetrate deep into the lungs if inhaled. It is better to try and prevent dust in your work space, rather than control it, so follow these guidelines carefully.

- **Work in a ventilated room, with easy-to-clean surfaces and facilities for washing nearby.**
- **Keep plastic clay damp and store dry powders in airtight containers.**
- **Floors should be kept clean and vacuumed at the end of the day – do not dry-sweep, as this will raise dust into the air.**
- **Wash down surfaces and clean tools at the end of a working day.**
- **When casting make sure that drips of slip are wiped from the surface of the mould and not allowed to dry out.**
- **Clean up any spillages before they dry out.**
- **Wear a facemask and goggles when turning, sanding or working with dry materials.**
- **Wear gloves when using colouring agents or oxides.**
- **Do not eat, drink or smoke in the work area.**
- **Always wash your hands thoroughly with soap before leaving the workshop and particularly before eating, drinking or smoking.**
- **Make sure you have an up to date tetanus immunization; raw clay comes from the ground and may contain bacteria.**

Toxic materials

Some of the materials that are used in ceramics to colour the clay or in glazes can be very highly toxic. Always carefully read the manufacturer's health and safety information given on containers and always wear the recommended protective clothing since recent research has shown that some materials may even be absorbed through the skin. If you take the proper precautions there should be no danger – but don't ignore safety issues just because you can only work for short periods at a time. Your general health is more important than achieving a quick result!

Lead, cadmium, antimony and barium are all very highly toxic, but are sometimes used in glazes. Lead gives a brilliance to the glaze and allows it to mature in the hobby firing range. Cadmium is essential to produce brilliant reds and yellows. Antimony can be used to make glaze more opaque, barium gives denser, more brilliant colour. Use extra-special care when handling anything containing these materials.

The following materials should be handled with some caution: ball clay, borax, boric acid, boron, china clay, chromium oxide, cobalt carbonate, cobalt oxide, copper carbonate, copper oxide, dolomite, feldspar, flint, quartz, silica, whiting.

If your item is intended to hold food or drink, check that the glaze you are using is certified food-safe and make sure you follow the firing instructions carefully. If the glaze is not fired correctly it may not mature or the surface may craze, which can mean that the final item will not be food safe.

pinch pots

Pinching is one of the most basic ways of making your first pot and is a very easy and quick technique to learn. It is an ideal way to start getting a feel for clay and to begin to understand its possibilities and its limits. To make several equal size pots, weigh the clay into equal amounts first.

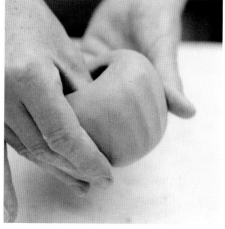

1 Break off a piece of soft clay and squeeze roughly into a smooth ball that fits comfortably in the palm of the hand. Use the thumb of the other hand to press down firmly into the centre of the ball, until you can feel the pressure on the palm holding the ball.

2 Rotate the clay, pinching the walls between your finger and thumb. Keep pinching the walls upwards and outwards, working from the base of the ball. Keep the rim quite thick until you are ready to make your final shape.

3 Pinch out the walls of the bowl, keeping them even. Keep working, making the walls thinner as you go until you achieve your final shape.

4 Pat the base of the bowl with a wooden spatula to make a base. Smooth the surfaces of your bowl with a flexible kidney.

5 Let the bowl dry completely, then bisque fire it as described on page 12, following the firing recommendations for the clay used.

6 To glaze the bowl see glazing techniques on pages 17–19. Glaze fire according to the glaze manufacturer's instructions.

Designer: Alex Hagen

texture & colour

To decorate your project you may want to add texture, colour, or a combination of both, to the surface. Texture is normally applied when the clay is still wet – you can either impress a design into the surface or add relief designs with a technique such as slip trailing or by applying cut-out clay motifs. Colour can be added either by glazing or by applying coloured slip. Both of these techniques can either be used to create an overall plain background colour, or to add a decorative design.

The range of different decoration that can be applied to ceramics is so wide that it would fill an entire book in itself, so here we have tried to concentrate on only the basic techniques. Don't be afraid to experiment and combine different techniques to get the final effect that you want.

1 Texture and shapes

You can use a variety of items to stamp a design into the surface of wet clay – you do not have to limit yourself to stamps. Try ordinary household or found items, such as wallpaper, dried pulses, leaves, shells… For cutting shapes you can use any small cutter – such as a biscuit cutter – to cut out shapes from the side of your form when it is leather hard. See step 7 on page 24 for information on using stamps and step 14 on page 141 for cutting out shapes.

2 Slip trailing

Another method of decorating is slip trailing using clay slip. Slip can be coloured with oxides, so it will add colour as well as texture. Slip trailing is done on wet clay. Fill the rubber bulb of the slip trailer with your slip then trail decorative lines along your clay, squeezing the bulb gently and evenly.

Glazing

Glazing can either be used to waterproof your project or to add colour and design. The clay form must be bisque fired before it is glazed. If you only want to waterproof your pot, you can just glaze inside and leave the outside in its natural state. For information on using transfers, see page 145.

Glaze preparation

Make sure your fired ceramic is totally dust free before you start glazing otherwise it will effect the surface of the glaze finish. You can make your own glazes, or you can buy powdered glazes. Mix the glaze according to the manufacturer's instructions. Sieve the glaze well before using it (usually at least twice through a 120 mesh sieve).

Technique 1: Pour glazing

1 Hold the item over another container, and pour the glaze over it.

2 Turn the item around and pour glaze over any missing areas. Allow to dry, then wipe the foot ring clean of glaze. With a dry finger, rub the seam line to smooth.

Technique 2: Dip Glazing

1 To dip glaze, dip the item halfway into the glaze. Allow to touch dry. Ensure that you have enough volume of glaze for this process.

2 Turn the item around and dip the other half up to the seam line of the previous dipping.

3 Allow to dry, then wipe the foot ring clean of any remaining glaze.

Smooth and creamy

Glaze does tend to settle quickly, so stir before use. Don't stir too vigorously or you will introduce air bubbles. Sieve your glaze with a 120-gauge sieve to make sure there are no lumps and it is perfectly smooth.

Stains can be added to glaze, underglaze or slip to add colour, and can also be mixed to produce other colours.

When firing it will help to even out bubbles and mature the glaze properly if you hold the top temperature for 10–30 minutes (depending on glaze and clay type). This is known as a 'soak' and can be programmed into your kiln controller.

Technique 3: Brush-on Glazing

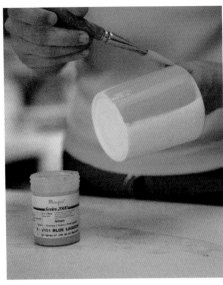

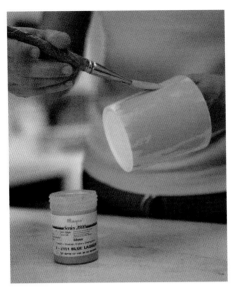

4 With a dry finger, rub over the seam line to smooth it down a little.

1 Brush-on glazes can be bought in small pots in a range of colours and are very stable. Stir well before use – add water if they have dried out. Make sure your item is dust free, then brush on using a soft brush.

2 Work all around the item, trying to keep the brushstrokes as even as possible. Leave to dry. Brush on a second coat. Follow the manufacturer's instructions for the number of coats.

coiling

Coiling is one of the traditional ways of creating pots
and it is very simple to master, although you will need
to practice to achieve evenly rolled coils. Despite its
simplicity the technique can be used to create quite
complex shapes. The coils can be left as visible as you
choose in the final project, or blended together to
achieve a smooth, flat surface.

In the round

Clay for coiling needs to be malleable.

Coil on cloth or newspaper, not on a hard surface, to stop the clay sticking.

Make the coils as you use them, or make them all in advance and keep them well wrapped in plastic until needed to prevent them drying out.

Light pressure is best as you are coiling – if you press too hard on the coils they will go into an oval rather than staying round.

Try looking away from the coil as you roll it, so you are rolling by touch not by sight. This often makes it easier to achieve round coils.

If the clay is soft it will stick together easily as you coil. If it has dried out a little you may need some slip to join the coils together.

Try not to work the clay too much with your hands when you are hand building a form, as the heat will dry it out quicker.

When coiling a pot, try not to make the walls thicker than 2.5cm (1in). Thicker clay is more prone to air bubbles.

1 Making a former

Cover a small earthenware or plastic plant pot, or some other former, with a layer of newspaper to prevent the clay sticking.

2 Rolling the coils

Wedge or knead the clay as described on page 8. Break off a piece of soft clay and squeeze roughly into a sausage shape. Flatten the ends so they don't flap about. Start rolling from the centre with your fingers spread out. You can make your coil any thickness you like – for this 10cm (4in) pot we have the coils around 1cm (½in) thick.

3 Start to coil shape

Cut a length of coil and start coiling around your form, trimming ends and pressing so they fit together. Start the second coil away from the join of the first as if the joins line up it may cause instability in the pot. You can coil in a spiral instead.

4 Pressing coils together

Press each layer of coils gently down to the previous one as you go. Keep the coils close together because you don't want any air bubbles that would cause the pot to explode in the kiln.

5 Making the base

To make the base, coil in a spiral on top of your form.

6 Smoothing

Start smoothing the coils together with your hands, then finish smoothing with a kidney tool. For the final smoothing it will help to have the pot on a turntable, so you can work on the whole pot at once rather than just on one side.

7 Pressing a design

Let the pot dry until not quite leather hard then press a design into the side. You can use a stamp or anything that will make an interesting pattern. Turn the pot right way up when you create the design – or remember you are working upside down.

8 Removing the former

Remove the former before the pot is dry – the clay shrinks slightly as it dries, so don't leave the former in too long. If some newspaper is left inside the pot leave it to be burnt off in the kiln or gently pull it out so you can smooth the inside.

Shapes

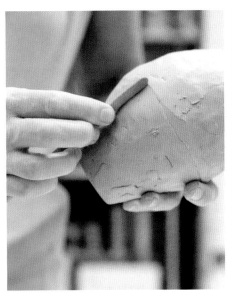

1 Joining shapes

Score both edges of the shapes before joining and paint on a little clay slip. You can add a thin coil of clay along the join to reinforce it.

2 Finishing off

Smooth the clay gently with your fingers until the join is invisible. Sponge the surface to finish.

Making curves

To make shaped sides, start coiling to a narrow diameter, then gradually make the diameter of your coils wider. When smoothing the sides, be careful not to press too hard or you will destroy the symmetry of the curves.

easy

★

heart pot

Personalizing your own flowerpots is both fun and simple and they make ideal gifts – particularly if you add a homegrown plant. Everyone loves a pot and they will all be impressed with your creative skills. It is always satisfying to make something that is practical and can be loved and used every day.

designer: Helen Johannessen

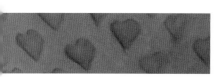

Materials

Earthenware clay
Plant pot, or some other
    former
Newspaper
Knife
Kidney tool
Stamp or found object
Sponge
Glaze (optional)

1 Cover the former with a layer of newspaper to prevent the clay sticking.

2 Make a coil from some of the earthenware clay as described in step 2 on page 22. Cut an appropriate length of coil and start coiling around your form, trimming the ends and pressing them so they fit together.

Potting up

This terracotta pot is exactly the same material as those you get in a garden centre – but is much more beautiful.

Pots can be coiled freeform – starting with the base and working upwards – but using a former means you will get a more even shape.

3 Carry on up the sides of your former until you reach the top.

4 To make the base, coil in a spiral on top of your form. Leave a hole in the centre for drainage – since the pot is unglazed terracotta it will also be porous.

5 Smooth the coils together as described in step 6 on page 24.

6 Let the clay stiffen slightly until it is less soft but not leather hard, then press your design into the side of the pot using a stamp or found object.

7 Remove the former before the pot is dry. If some newspaper is left inside the pot leave it to be burnt off in the kiln or gently pull it out so you can smooth the inside. Sponge off around the top to smooth the edge.

8 Bisque fire the pot to 1000ºC, as described on page 12.

9 There is no need to glaze the pot, but if you do want to, see glazing techniques on pages 17–19, then glaze fire following the instructions for your chosen glaze.

advanced
★★★

aperture

My work is based on an exploration of the relationship between shape, volume and negative space and I draw ideas from the organic and natural. Although this vase is functional its sculptural context is more important – I like to create a sense of movement, balance and harmony in every individual piece.

designer: Tina Vlassopulos

Materials

Stoneware clay
Bat
Potter's knife
Soft pencil
Kitchen scourer
Turntable
Serrated metal kidney
Metal kidney
Boxwood rib
Old spoon or pebble for
  burnishing
Piece of plastic

See also

Making curves on page 25.
Cutting out shapes in step 14
  on page 141.

1 Follow steps 1–6 for coiling on pages 22–24. Start by making a base inside a drop-out mould (see pages 98–99) or with a pinch pot (see pages 14–15). If you use a pinch pot, place it on a sponge to stop it being distorted out of shape as you work.

2 Start coiling the body of your vase, from the base upwards. You can make your coils any thickness you like, but here they are quite thick so that there is enough clay to scrape and smooth the walls at the end. Trim the ends of the coils and press them so they fit together. Blend each layer of coils as you go.

3 Start wider at the base and narrow the sides slightly as you move upwards, to start creating the in-and-out curves of the sides.

4 Start opening out the vase again, then narrow the sides slightly again as you reach the top.

5 Allow the pot to dry a little, but do not allow it to become leather hard. Cut the rim, then mark the shape of the slot with a soft pencil and cut it out with a potter's knife. Smooth the cut edges with the kitchen scourer.

6 For the final smoothing it will help to have the pot on a turntable, so you can work on the whole pot at once rather than just on one side. Start scraping with a serrated kidney and then with a metal kidney to smooth the surface.

7 Finally use a boxwood rib to smooth the surface even further.

8 Let the vase dry until it is leather hard.

9 Burnish the surface with a pebble or an old spoon, working over it at least three times until it is hard and shiny. Finally wrap your finger in a piece of plastic and go over the surface one more time to achieve a rich sheen.

10 Bisque fire (see page 12) the vase to a maximum of 960°C.

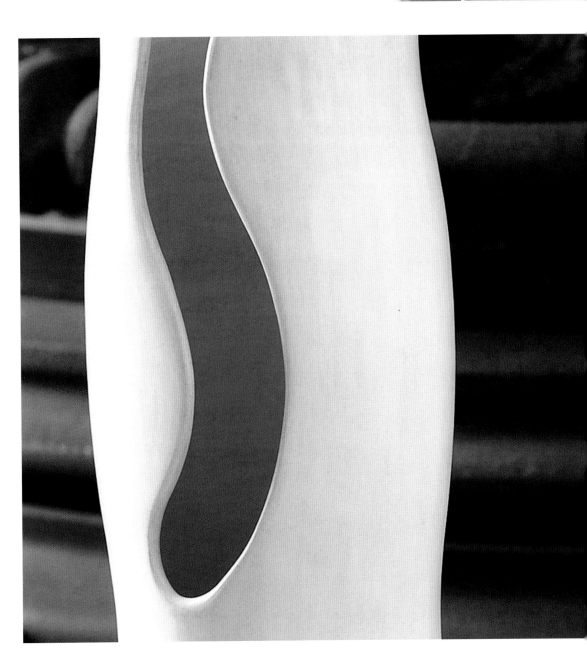

advanced
★★★

abstract curves

The smooth, bulbous curves of this shape contrast beautifully with the sharply defined lines of the edges. The abstract shape with its three main sections can be positioned in different ways, giving a changing look to the sculpture. The shadows and spaces between the shapes add an extra dimension to the design.

designer: Merete Rasmussen

Materials

Earthstone hand-building clay
Bat
Potter's knife
Plastic sheet
Clay supports
Foam
Clay slip
Serrated steel metal kidney
   tool
Plastic kidney tool
Turntable
Fine grade sandpaper
Coloured slip

1 Roll out a coil with your hands on a clean bench. Follow the steps for coiling on pages 22–25, working on a bat. You can make your coil any thickness you like – for this sculptural shape the coils are around 2cm (⅞in) thick.

2 Start coiling the base of the first bowl shape. Start building the walls up quite quickly from the base to create the rounded bottom.

3 Trim the ends of the coils and press them so they fit together. Press each layer of coils gently down to the previous one as you go. Keep the coils close together.

4 As you get to the size of bowl shape you need, start twisting the coils in opposite directions to create the 'arms' that will be used to join the bowl shapes together.

5 Smooth the coils together with your fingers then sponge the surface. Cover with plastic and set aside.

6 Make two more bowl shapes by repeating steps 1 to 5 twice.

7 Use the 'arms' to join the shapes and create the sculptural form shown, supporting the sections with clay supports and foam if necessary. Score edges before joining and paint on a little clay slip. Smooth the joins with your fingers until they are invisible.

8 When you have made the basic shape, allow it to dry until it is leather hard. Work on the surface with the serrated metal kidney to even it, then use the plastic kidney until it is perfectly smooth.

9 Let the form dry completely, then bisque fire it at 950°C as described on page 12, resting the form on a spare slab of clay to prevent uneven shrinkage during the firing process.

10 After firing, sand the form with fine sandpaper to remove any blemishes on the surface.

11 To finish, spray with an even layer of coloured slip, then fire to 1200°C.

Shapeshifting

Make sure all the surfaces
are as smooth as possible
before bisque firing,
because this will mean
less work when fettling.

There is no need to glaze
this project as the
coloured slip will vitrify
when fired.

intermediate

★★

stoneware bottles

Simplicity and stillness are qualities that inspire my work. Within stillness, I find movement in asymmetry and imperfection, for example in the gentle undulating line of a rim. This set that consists of two bottles is relational – I am interested in the dialogue between outlines of the two shapes when seen next to each other.

designer: Alex Hagen

Materials

Stoneware clay
Bat
Turntable
Water
Kidney tool
Modelling tool
Dolomite glaze

1 Break off a piece of soft clay and squeeze roughly into a sausage shape. Follow steps 1–6 for coiling on pages 22–24, but work on a bat from the base upwards. You can make your coil any thickness you like – for these bottles the coils are made around 1.5cm (⅝in) thick.

2 Cut an appropriate length of coil and start making the base by coiling a spiral to the width of the bottle.

3 Put the base on a turntable and start coiling the body of your bottle, trimming the ends of the coils and pressing them so they fit well together. Start wider at the base and work inwards slightly as you move upwards.

4 Press each layer of coils gently down to the previous one as you go.

5 Start smoothing the coils together with your hands both on the inside and the outside of the bottle. Then narrow the coiling to make the neck of the bottle.

6 When you have finished the bottle shape, smooth the remaining coils together with your fingers. Trim and smooth the edge.

7 When the clay is leather hard, use the kidney tool to further smooth the surface of the bottle. With the modelling tool finish the sharply angled bevel at the base of the neck.

8 Let the bottle dry completely, then bisque fire it at 1000ºC as described on page 12.

9 To glaze the bottle see glazing techniques on pages 17–19 and fire glaze according to recommendations for your chosen glaze.

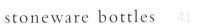

slabbing

Slabbing is one of the basic construction techniques for ceramics; it allows the maker to create both simple and complex forms. It is worth spending time practicing the technique to avoid problems with construction and firing at later stages.

1 Pounding clay

Place a piece of wedged clay (see page 8) onto a plastic sheet. Beat the clay with the rolling pin using evenly weighted strokes, working from one side to another and slightly twisting the pin as you make contact to prevent it from sticking to the clay. Turn the clay over, twist round by 90° and repeat this process on the other side to create an evenly shaped block. This technique will help to get rid of any air that may be trapped in the clay and help you roll an evenly shaped slab.

2 Rolling

Position the roller guides on either side of the block of clay – they will hold the rolling pin off the surface to set the final thickness of the slab and keep it even. Starting from the centre, roll the clay away from your body then roll back, trying to keep an even pressure on the rolling pin. After a while the clay will start to build a slight resistance to rolling – this is an indication that it is time to turn the slab over and work on the other side.

3 Peeling

Lift the slab by picking up the piece of plastic then turn it over so the slab rests on your other hand. Carefully peel away the plastic from the clay and place the plastic back onto the table – don't pull at the clay to get it off the plastic as this may tear or distort the slab. Gently place the slab back onto the plastic the other way up, and turn through 90° before rolling again, using the guides as before. Rolling slabs this way prevents any rips or tears in the clay.

4 Adding texture

You can add texture to the surface of your clay by impressing almost anything into the surface while it is still soft. Stamps or found objects such as buttons, leaves or shells can be used for individual motifs. Textured wallpaper is great to create an overall pattern – lay it textured side down on the clay with the roller guides still in place and roll over it firmly, pressing it down into the surface. Lift a corner and peel off carefully to avoid smudging the design.

5 Cutting shapes

To cut shapes from your slab you can use a variety of items, but biscuit and pastry cutters are ideal. Press the cutter firmly into the clay, right down to the surface beneath. The shape will probably come away from the slab inside the cutter, so you can gently press it out to one side.

handkerchief soap dish

I am inspired by the simple things in life – home, fun, family. This quirky porcelain soap dish gets its name from the soft 'folded' look that it shares with old-fashioned cloth handkerchiefs. It and the matching toothbrush holder on page 50 are decorated with vintage stamps and glazed in pastel colours. I use porcelain, but you can use any clay – the toothbrush holder in particular is easier to make using stoneware or earthenware clay.

designer: Jo Heckett

Materials

Porcelain clay
Plastic sheet
Rolling pin
Roller guides
Potter's knife
Potter's needle
Small cutters about 1cm
  (⅜in) in diameter
Stamps
Pen or pencil
Sponge
Transparent stoneware glaze
Glaze stains

See also

pressing a design in step 7
  on page 24.

1 Prepare your clay slab as described in steps 1–3 on pages 44–45. It should be at least 14 x 18cm (5½ x 7¼in) and approximately 5mm (¼in) thick. Make sure the clay is quite soft and floppy when forming, as if it is too dry at this stage it may crack in the kiln.

2 Cut the soap dish to 11 x 15.5cm (4¼ x 6¼in), or the dimensions of your choice. Porcelain clay will shrink about 10–15% during firing.

3 Mark the positions of the drainage holes using a knife or needle. Cut the drainage holes using a small cutter – it should be around 1cm (⅜in) in diameter.

4 Stamp the design in the flat part of the soap dish as shown in step 7 on page 24, avoiding the drainage holes.

5 To shape the edges of the soap dish, carefully fold up one side at a time and support each one with a pen, pencil or similar placed along and slightly under each edge to prevent it falling back down or cracking. Work carefully and quickly, supporting the lifted edges at all times. Pay special attention to the corners.

6 Wrap the dish loosely in thin plastic sheeting and leave the finished piece to completely dry.

7 When dry, carefully smooth the edges with a well wrung out, slightly damp sponge. Do this very gently as unfired clay is easily broken.

8 Bisque fire the dish to 1060°C if using porcelain, or to the appropriate temperature for your clay, as described on page 12.

9 To glaze the dish, see glazing techniques on pages 17–19. The project shown features transparent stoneware glaze with added glaze stains. Glaze fire to 1250°C, or to the appropriate temperature for the clay and glaze used.

Child's play

When looking for small cutters, try those designed for cutting children's modelling clay.

Before firing, make sure the base is completely free of all glaze residue, and remember to remove any extra glaze from around the bottom edge of the drainage holes.

intermediate

★★

vintage toothbrush holder

Working in the finest porcelain, I use a quirky mix of found objects, vintage printing stamps, and letters to stamp into the surface. Each of my pieces is lovingly produced, with great attention to detail, and made to be enjoyed. This toothbrush holder matches the soap dish on page 46.

designer: Jo Heckett

Materials

Porcelain clay
Plastic sheet
Rolling pin
Roller guides
Potter's knife or scalpel
Cookie cutter about 9cm
   (3½in) in diameter
Small cutter about 1cm (⅜in)
   in diameter (optional)
Stamps
White vinegar
Small paintbrush
Large cardboard roll
   (optional)
Newspaper (optional)
Modelling tool
Sponge
Transparent stoneware glaze
Glaze stains

See also

pressing a design in step 7
   on page 24
joining shapes in step 1 on
   page 25.

1 Prepare your clay slab as described in steps 1–3 on pages 44–45, making it at least 32 x 15cm (13 x 6in) and approximately 6mm (¼in) thick. Make sure the clay is quite soft and floppy when forming, as if it is too dry at this stage it is likely to crack in the kiln or while drying.

2 Cut a rectangular section of slab to 28 x 11cm (11½ x 4½in), to make the sides of the holder, and a round piece using the cookie cutter about 9cm (3½in) in diameter to make the base. Porcelain clay will shrink about 10–15% during firing. Use a small cutter to cut drainage holes in the round base if you prefer.

3 Stamp the design in the sides of the rectangular slab, as described in step 7 on page 24. If you wish, carefully turn the slab and repeat along the inside of the rim on the other side of the slab.

4 Using a scalpel or knife score the short edges of the rectangle in a cross hatching fashion as well as the long edge at the bottom edge and the outermost 6mm (¼in) of the round piece of slab. Be careful not to actually slice into the clay. The aim is to go no deeper than a millimetre.

5 Apply vinegar to the scored short edges using a small paintbrush and join carefully. If necessary use a cardboard roll or piece of plastic pipe of the right thickness to form the holder around – first tape a double layer of newspaper loosely around it so the cup slips off easily after forming.

6 Push the scored edges together firmly but gently until the vinegar begins to ooze out. Use your finger or a modelling tool to seal the join and smooth it down on both sides of the join. Make sure you support the opposite side of the join at all times.

7 Now apply vinegar to the scored bottom edge of the holder and the scored area of the base and firmly but carefully press together. Smooth the join as in step 5.

8 Wrap the holder loosely in thin plastic sheeting and leave the finished piece to dry slowly until completely dry.

9 When dry, carefully smooth the edges with a well wrung out, slightly damp sponge. Do this very gently as unfired clay is easily broken.

10 Bisque fire as described on page 12, to 1060°C if using porcelain or the appropriate temperature for your clay.

11 To glaze the toothbrush holder, see glazing techniques on pages 17–19. The project shown features transparent stoneware glaze with added glaze stains. Glaze fire to 1250°C, or to the appropriate temperature for your clay and glaze.

botanical wall plaques

Inspiration for these wall plaques is drawn from the country garden where seasonal organic specimens are also gathered to impress into the clay. Leaves, flowers, seed heads, grasses and even weeds can be used to great effect, so you should always be able to find samples no matter where you live.

designer: Charlie Atkin

Materials

White firing stoneware clay
Plastic sheet
Rolling pin
Roller guides
Botanical sample
Potter's knife
Hole cutter
Selection of body stains
Stoneware reactive/opalescent
    glaze

1 Prepare your clay slab as described in steps 1–3 on pages 44–45. The slab can be any size as more than one plaque can be cut from it – and it should be 5–10mm (¼–½in) thick depending on the thickness of the specimen to be impressed into it.

2 Allow the clay to dry a little. Lay the flower sample on top of the slab and roll it into the surface using the rolling pin to make an interesting textured pattern in the clay.

3 Cut the plaque from the slab, making sure your pressed pattern is placed in the centre. The size of the plaque will be dictated by the impressed sample. Make a hanging hole at the top with a hole cutter.

4 Leave the finished piece to completely dry, turning regularly to make sure that it dries flat.

5 Bisque fire the wall plaques to 1000°C, as described on page 12.

6 Paint the impressions with a selection of body stain colours then wipe back carefully to make sure that the colours remain in the texture only.

7 To glaze the wall plaques see glazing techniques on pages 17–19 or alternatively, sponge the glaze over the plaque using a natural sponge for a slightly mottled effect. Glaze fire to 1260°C.

intermediate
★★

porcelain paperclay nightlight

I am inspired by nature and I enjoy inlaying a range of natural textures into porcelain paperclay to create unusual and subtle lighting effects. When illuminated the light shines through the translucent paperclay and the pattern of the textures is accentuated on the surface of the clay.

designer: Liz Emtage

Materials

Porcelain paperclay
Plastic sheet
Rolling pin
Roller guides
Pin or needle
Stamp or found object
Craft knife
Cardboard cylinder or paper
    cup
Newspaper (optional)
Clay slip
Paintbrush
Modelling tool
High-firing opaque glaze of
    your choice
Tealight

See also

pressing a design in step 7
    on page 24.

1 Prepare and roll your slab as described in steps 1–3 on pages 44–45. Start with rolling guides in place and then remove them to roll your clay as thin as you dare. Because you are using paperclay it can be worked much thinner than clay alone. Roll to approximately 3mm (⅛ in) thick, aiming to keep the clay the same thickness all over. Test the thickness with a pin/needle.

2 Press a design into the surface of the slab as described in step 4 on page 45, or use a stamp or found object as shown in step 7 on page 24. Take care to remove all non-organic items before firing.

3 Cut a section of slab to fit around your former – the slab needs to be a little bigger so there is 1cm (⅜ in) for joining and so it will slide off the former. You can also wrap the former in newspaper so the clay will not stick to it.

4 Roll the slab around the former to make a cylinder. Where the joins overlap, score and paint a little slip on one side and then join together. Make sure you allow enough space between the former and its clay jacket so it can be removed easily.

5 Use a paintbrush and a tiny amount of water to smooth over the joins on the inside and outside.

6 Place the cylinder on a piece of spare slab and cut out around the base with a sharp knife, making the base very slightly larger to allow for the join.

7 Join the base to the cylinder with some slip and a paintbrush.

8 Check the stamped design and touch up if required at the joins. Smooth the rim and leave the finished cylinder to completely dry.

9 Bisque fire the lamp to 1000°C, as described on page 12.

10 To glaze the lamp see glazing techniques on pages 17–19, then glaze fire to 1260°C. Try out different glazes for colour and transparency.

11 Place a tealight inside the lamp.

A little light music

You can buy paperclay ready mixed or you can make your own. Experiment with different clays and quantities of paper to clay – but remember you should always have more paper to clay in the mix.

See what new patterns you can create using everyday objects, Try screw heads, pen lids, paperclips, scissors – the list is endless.

If you don't want a flame in your light you can now buy battery-powered tealights on the Internet.

Experiment making different sized lamps to see the different lights they produce.

easy

★

wind chime

This is a great project that can be made with minimal making skills on your kitchen table. Inspired by the countryside in which I live and contemporary textures in current fashions and trends, this wind chime was created using porcelain clay, which when fired high has a perfect sound and translucency for this type of project.

designer: Charlie Atkin

Materials

Porcelain and black
  stoneware clay
Plastic sheet
Rolling pin
Roller guides
Textured wallpaper or lace
Large circular cutter
Leaf shaped biscuit cutters
Potter's knife
Hole cutter
Lengths of fine cord
Brass ring

1 Prepare your clay slab as described in steps 1–3 on pages 44–45. Make the slab as large as possible to cut all sections required, and no thicker than 5mm (¼in) although remember it will roll thinner when textured.

2 Place the slab over a sheet of textured wallpaper then place another sheet of paper over the top. Re-roll the slab so that both sides are impressed.

3 Using the biscuit cutters, cut out six leaf shapes from the slab. If you don't have a suitable cutter you can draw the outline of a leaf and cut it out with a potter's knife. Make sure you cut an equal amount of black and white leaves to balance out the wind chime – three black, three white.

4 Using the circular cutter, cut out a disk 15cm (6in) in diameter from the slab.

5 With the hole cutter, make six hanging holes equally spaced around the edge of the disk. Make one hanging hole in the top of each leaf shape.

6 Leave the leaves and the disk to completely dry – it does not matter if they curl a little in the drying process as this makes the leaves more realistic.

7 Fire the leaves and the disk slowly to a top temperature of 1260°C – there is no need to bisque fire because the items are unglazed.

8 Assemble the wind chime by threading a length of thin cord through each of the holes on the disk and knotting them together at the top through the brass ring. Make a knot in the cord below each hole in the disk hold it in position. Thread and knot the leaves on at varying heights so they hang in a spiral.

wind chime 65

throwing

To master the technique of throwing requires a
great deal of practice. Don't be discouraged – once
conquered this method of working with clay can be
hugely rewarding and produce spectacular results.
Makers use many methods to throw pots and to avoid
confusion only one method is illustrated here in great
detail. It is well worth taking a few lessons in this
particular technique to help you master it more easily.
This should also give you access to a wheel and a kiln
until you are ready to invest in your own equipment.

Throwing a Bowl

Roundabout

Clay for throwing needs to be quite soft and malleable.

Keep your arms tucked into your sides and supported on the edge of the tray as your clay form rises, as it is more likely to wobble as it gets taller.

Before shaping the base and cutting the foot ring, make sure your bowl is centred on the wheel or turntable.

Don't put too much water on the bat or the ball of clay will not stick.

1 Kneading

Thoroughly knead the clay to even out the body and remove any air bubbles. This process also redistributes the moisture in the material. Push down on the clay with the heel of your hand while moving it forwards, rotate the clay and repeat.

2 Centring

Dampen the bat and throw the clay ball down on the centre, making sure it's firmly in position. Gently tap the clay to the centre of the bat. With the wheel moving slowly, cup the clay between your hands and pull it slightly towards your body to centre it completely on the wheel.

3 Wet the clay

Sprinkle the clay with a little water to get it started and begin moving the wheel faster. With the wheel moving swiftly, cup the clay with your hands and squeeze inwards using your thumb on top of the clay to exert pressure downwards.

4 Opening

With the wheel still moving swiftly, press your thumbs into the centre of the clay. Press to within around 4cm (1½in) of the base of your bowl and then push the clay out sideways to widen the form.

5 Lifting the wall

With your fingers inside the bowl and your thumb gripping the outside wall, begin lifting the wall of the bowl by squeezing the thumb and fingers of your hand together, while keeping the wheel moving at a constant speed. Make a groove near the base of the clay with your thumb.

6 Shaping

The final shape of the bowl is formed by using the throwing rib. Start just above the base of the bowl and use the rib on the outside of the bowl, supporting the inside of the bowl with your thumb. The final stages of the shaping should be made with the wheel moving very slowly.

7 Smoothing

The sides of the bowl will still have rings made during the throwing process. Smooth these away using a metal kidney, with the wheel turning quite slowly.

8 Cutting off

To remove the bowl from the wheel, first cut around the outer edge of the base of the pot with a potter's knife. Flood the wheel head with water, then carefully slide the cutting wire under the base of the bowl, keeping it taut between your fingers and flat to the wheel head.

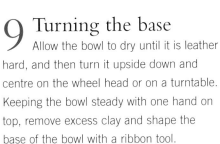

9 Turning the base

Allow the bowl to dry until it is leather hard, and then turn it upside down and centre on the wheel head or on a turntable. Keeping the bowl steady with one hand on top, remove excess clay and shape the base of the bowl with a ribbon tool.

10 Cutting the foot ring

Use the ribbon tool to cut away the centre of the bottom of the bowl and define the inside edge of the foot ring. Smooth the area inside the foot ring with a wooden modelling tool or a sponge.

Throwing a Cylinder

Straight up

A cylinder is the basis of many tall thin shapes, but is slightly more complex than throwing a bowl as it is more likely to wobble as it grows taller.

Try throwing a series of cylinders using the same amount of clay each time – you will be able to measure your progress and throwing accuracy by comparing them.

For a more finished look to your cylinder, try leaving the rim a little thicker than the walls.

Cylinders can be used as chucks – forms to hold a pot upside-down above the wheel head while it is trimmed. Chucks are thrown and bisque-fired clay cylinders open on both sides.

Cut the cylinder off the wheel head as described in step 8 on page 70. You should not need to trim the base.

1 Opening up

Prepare the clay as in steps 1–3 on pages 68–69. With the wheel still moving swiftly, press your thumbs into the centre of the clay to within around 5mm (¼in) of the wheel head. Push the clay out sideways with your thumb to widen the form.

2 Lifting the wall

With your fingers inside and your thumb gripping the outside wall, begin lifting the wall of the cylinder by squeezing the thumb and fingers of your hand together, while keeping the wheel moving at a constant speed. Make a groove near the base of the clay with your thumb.

3 Pulling up

With your left fingers inside, push out a small bulge at the base of the cylinder. Gently move the bulge up the side with the fingers or knuckle of your other hand, while the fingers inside continue to push outwards. The bulge should move up to the top of the cylinder in one smooth motion.

4 Smoothing

Repeat the pulling up action as described in step 3 several times to create the full height of your cylinder. Use your index finger to smooth the rim. Smooth off the throwing rings as described in step 7 on page 70.

Throwing a Plate

Discus throwing

Plates and other flat forms are often thrown on a bat, because they are hard to remove from the wheel head when they are still wet. When you have finished throwing, cut the plate off the bat with the cutting wire as described in step 8 on page 70, but then leave it on the bat to dry. When the plate is dry enough not to distort when handled, wire again and transfer to a dry surface.

You can leave extra clay under the rim of your plate to support it until the clay is hard enough to remain stable. Cut the extra clay away with a ribbon tool when the plate is leather hard.

Turn the base of your plate and a foot ring as described in steps 9 and 10 on page 71.

The middle of the base of your plate should dip slightly so it stands only on the outside edge when it is fired. Cut a little clay away from the centre with a ribbon tool, reducing the depth of your cut as you reach the edge.

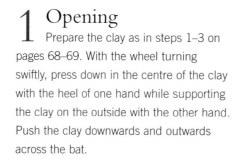

1 Opening
Prepare the clay as in steps 1–3 on pages 68–69. With the wheel turning swiftly, press down in the centre of the clay with the heel of one hand while supporting the clay on the outside with the other hand. Push the clay downwards and outwards across the bat.

2 Pressing the centre
The small rise in the centre of the plate is flattened out by pressing with the side of your hand, moving the hand slowly towards the edge. Repeat several times. Consolidate the clay on the base by pressing down with your fingers moving from the centre to the edge.

3 Forming the rim

With the thumb of one hand under the rim, place the fingers on the inside supported by the fingers of the other hand. Squeeze gently to consolidate the clay on the rim, then slowly draw the clay outwards and upwards.

4 Finishing off

Use a throwing rib to smooth the base of the plate, working from the centre outwards and applying gentle pressure. Remove excess water with a sponge. Use the rib to create a bevel underneath the plate as a guide for the cutting wire.

intermediate
★★

bud vase

Since I began making there have always been pots for flowers – some larger, some smaller and some for a single stem. This pot is the latest variation on the theme...

designer: Chris Keenan

Materials

Porcelain clay
Rib tool
Wheel
Water
Metal kidney
Stick
Ribbon tool
Sponge
High-firing stoneware glaze˙

1 For a vase that will be around 10–11cm (4–4¼in) in height after firing, prepare 225g (½lb) of porcelain clay as described on page 8. To throw a simple cylinder shape, begin by following the basic throwing steps on pages 72–73.

2 Begin lifting the wall. Place your thumb and hand at the base of the vase on the outside. Push the thumb in slightly to create a small hollow. Curl the rest of your hand over the rim of the pot to the inside and rest the other hand on the rim and over the first hand for support. Squeeze the finger and thumb of your hand together as the clay wall is lifted, maintaining the pressure as you get almost to the top.

3 As the cylinder rises, push it slightly to narrow the form, maintaining the position of your hand on the rim. Try to keep the wall thickness as even as possible.

4 With your fingers still inside the pot, push out slightly at the base. Keep the wheel moving all the time. Smooth out the throwing rings with the rib tool.

5 Remove the form from the bat or wheel head as shown in step 8 on page 70. Leave to become leather hard.

6 Put the vase back on wheel, centre it and turn to refine your desired shape. Turn the base as described in step 9 on page 71.

7 Dip the top half of the form in water to soften it slightly. Hit the vase firmly once with the end of the stick (the size of stick will depend on the size of your pot!) to create a clear indentation near the top. Smooth the rim to a shape you like.

8 Bisque fire the vase to 1000°, as described on page 12.

9 To glaze the vase see glazing techniques on pages 17–19. Use high-firing stoneware glazes that mature at around 1240–1260°C and glaze fire according to the recommendations for your chosen glaze.

advanced
★★★

spring green cup and saucer

Throwing is an ancient craft that has been around for thousands of years, but is still very contemporary. I like to feel that I am making something with a sense of tradition that will be used every day. This cup and saucer is thrown in stoneware, which is stronger than earthenware, and is glazed in a wonderful clear green.

designer: Katie Adams

Materials

Stoneware clay
Wheel
Water
Kidney tool
Cutting wire
Glaze of your choice

See also

pulling a handle in step 16 on
   page 153.

1 Start by wedging and then kneading the clay very thoroughly, as described on page 8, to mix it and remove any air bubbles.

2 Weigh out 340g (¾lb) of clay for the cup and 227g (½lb) for the saucer.

3 Throw the cup as described in the basic throwing steps 2–7 on pages 68–70. As you lift the wall, with your left hand turn your wrist so the pads of the three fingers on the inside and the supporting thumb on the outside create the curve of the lip.

4 Cut the cup off the wheel with a cutting wire as described in step 8 on page 70 and leave it to dry for 24 hours or until it is leather hard.

5 The following day, turn the cup over and carve the foot ring into the base, as described in step 10 on page 71.

6 Pull the handle from a sausage of firmer clay, as described in step 16 on page 153, and cut a section off to a suitable length.

7 Score the surface of the outer side of the cup slightly to mark the position of the handle and add a small amount of water with a paintbrush. Push the top of the handle into the side of the cup and work it firmly into position with your fingers.

8 Holding the cup in your hands with the handle dropping down vertically, flatten the top of the handle then curve it around in a nice shape and push the bottom end into the cup. Since the sides of the saucer are quite high, make sure the base of the handle will be high enough to clear them. Smooth the bottom end of the handle firmly into place with your fingers.

9 Throw the saucer at the same time as you make the cup so the drying time will be the same. Measure the diameter of the recess in the saucer that will take the cup as you work, so the two pieces will fit together. The recess should be around 6.5 cm in diameter.

10 Throw the saucer as shown in the basic throwing steps on pages 74–75, using your fingers to pull a big ridge out and down to make the sides of the saucer. Use a curved kidney tool to shape the curve of the saucer sides.

11 Cut the saucer off the wheel with a cutting wire, as described in step 8 on page 70, and leave it to dry for 24 hours.

12 The following day, turn the saucer over and carve the foot ring into the base, as described in step 10 on page 71.

13 Leave the saucer to dry thoroughly, which will take at least 24 hours.

14 Bisque fire both the cup and the saucer at the same time to 1000°C, as described on page 12.

15 To glaze the cup and saucer see glazing techniques on pages 17–19, then glaze fire to 1260°C or to the recommended instructions for your chosen glaze.

intermediate
★★

rocking bowls

This is a form that I first came across when I was apprenticed to Edmund de Waal. I love the fact that the lack of a flat base gives each individual piece a different character – no two stand in the same way and they can appear to be in communication when seen in larger groups. I don't ascribe a function to these pots but I know they are used for widely varying purposes incorporating both solids and liquids.

designer: Chris Keenan

Materials

Porcelain clay
Wheel
Water
Rib tool
Strip of chamois
Loop tool
Metal kidney
High-firing stoneware glaze

1 Prepare around 225–775g (½–1¾lb) of clay, depending on the size of bowl you want to achieve. To throw a basic bowl shape, begin by following the basic throwing steps 2–7 on pages 68–70. When forming the base of the rocking bowl do not flatten it but leave it concave inside.

2 Begin lifting the wall, following the curve of the base up into the wall. Place your thumb and hand at the base of the bowl on the outside. Push the thumb in slightly to create a deep hollow. Curl the rest of the hand over the rim of the bowl to the inside and rest the other hand on the rim and over the first hand for support. Squeeze the finger and thumb of your hand together as the clay wall is lifted, maintaining the pressure as you get almost to the top.

3 As the bowl rises, push it inwards to curve in at the top, maintaining the position of your hand on the rim. Try to keep the wall thickness as even as possible and leave plenty of clay around the base for cutting into later.

4 With each lift increase the curve of the wall as well as increasing the height of the bowl. Remember to squeeze in at the top of the bowl at the end of each lift to bring the rim back in – this is known as 'collaring'. The internal profile of this form is particularly important as this determines the final shape of the piece when it is turned.

5 The final shape of the bowl is formed by using the throwing rib. Start just above the base and use the rib on the outside of the bowl, supporting the inside of the bowl with your thumb. The final stages of the shaping should be made with the wheel moving very slowly. Use a strip of wet chamois to smooth out the rim.

6 Remove the form from the bat or wheel head as described in step 8 on page 70.

7 Allow the bowl to dry until it is leather hard. Turn it over and centre on the wheel head or place on a centred chuck, then use the loop tool to cut away excess clay on the bottom and create the rounded rocking base. Finally, using a metal kidney, smooth until you have achieved the surface finish you want.

8 Bisque fire the bowl to 1000°C, as described on page 12.

9 To glaze the bowl see glazing techniques on pages 17–19. Use high-firing stoneware glazes that mature at around 1240–1260°C and then wipe back the rim. Stand the bowl on its rim and glaze fire following recommendations for your chosen glaze.

intermediate
★★

porcelain
fruit bowl

This thrown bowl is made to contain fruit, but its pure simplicity of shape means that it stands alone as a decorative piece in its own right. My work is a constant attempt to balance proportion and shape, and to create forms with sense of presence and beauty.

Materials

Porcelain clay
Bat
Wheel
Water
Sponge
Rib tool
Glaze of your choice

1   To throw the bowl shape begin by following the basic throwing steps 1–6 on pages 68–70.

2   With your left hand fingers inside the bowl and your thumb gripping the outside wall, begin lifting the wall of the bowl by pressing the clay from both sides, while keeping the wheel moving. Make a round shape in the bottom of the bowl by pressing the clay.

3   The outside of the bowl is smoothed by using a metal rib. Starting from above the base of the bowl to the top, press the clay outside in using the rib, while the left hand fingers support the shape of the inside of the bowl.

4   Shape the rim of the bowl smoothly.

5   Remove the bowl from the bat as described in step 8 on page 70 and leave it to dry until it is leather hard.

6   Then, turn the bowl over and trim the foot ring into the base, as described in step 10 on page 71.

7   Leave the bowl to dry completely, then bisque fire to 1000°C, as described on page 12.

8   To glaze the bowl see glazing techniques on pages 17–19, then fire following the recommendations for your chosen glaze.

porcelain fruit bowl 91

mould making and slipcasting

If you want to copy a shape exactly, or make several identical forms, then making a mould is the ideal technique because you can then use it to create as many copies of your original model as you like. Mould making is a little more work to begin with, but afterwards it is quick and easy to slipcast from your mould.

Mixing Plaster

Plaster master

Keramicast plaster takes 15 minutes from mixing to setting, potter's plaster takes 10 minutes so don't work too slowly. It is useful to time your plaster because if you pour it too soon the final mould will be too soft.

Leave the powder to quench for one minute before you start mixing to be sure you won't have lumps.
When you are mixing keep your hand below the water level so you don't add air bubbles to the mix.

Make sure any dry bits of plaster around the edges of the bucket are mixed in or they will pour into your mould.

Make sure the walls of the mould are firm as the plaster is heavy and can make them bulge outwards. If necessary, add more layers of string. When you are disposing of excess plaster always pour it into a bin, never down the sink or it will block the pipes. Alternatively you can use left over plaster to make a plaster bat that can be used in other processes

1 Preparation

Use a clean bucket – make sure there is no debris inside or it will get into the plaster. Measure the cold water into the bucket and add the plaster to the water – never the other way round.

2 Adding the plaster

Scatter handfuls of plaster over the water – make sure all the powder is soaking into the water. The powder should start peaking above the water level when there is the correct plaster-to-water ratio. Leave to stand for a minute and then start mixing with your hand.

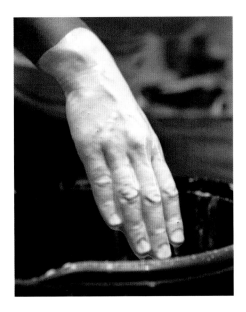

3 Checking consistency

To check the thickness pull your hand out – the plaster should be the consistency of double cream. It should drip a little but still coat your hand so that you cannot see the colour of your skin. The longer you mix, the more the water mixes into the plaster to start the chemical reaction of setting.

4 Pouring the plaster

Leave the plaster to stand until it starts to thicken – but watch carefully as once it starts to harden it will do so quickly. Pour the plaster into the mould – you have a window of about three minutes before it will be too hard. Tap the top of the plaster in the mould to bring up any air bubbles.

Turning Plaster

Round in circles

When working on the lathe, make sure the rest is as close to the plaster as possible so your fingers cannot go down between it and the lathe.

Turn as slowly as you feel comfortable – going too fast can be dangerous.

It is not necessary to have expensive tools for this process. Use inexpensive chisels from economy shops because using them on wet material will blunt them quite quickly.

There are specialist lathes for this process, but an old woodturning lathe will do the job – older heavy-duty equipment is often the best.

Draw up a full-scale drawing of your design to use as reference when turning the model on the lathe.

Make sure the securing string goes around up the full height of your cottle wall – plaster is heavy and it can start to push the wall outwards.

1 Preparing the lathe
Prepare the plate for the lathe by cutting in some grooves to create undercuts, so the fresh plaster will stick onto the lathe chuck (metal plate that holds the plaster to be turned).

2 Cottling
Place the plate on the chuck and wrap a sheet of thick vinyl around the whole thing – this is known as cottling. Secure the vinyl with string. Mix the plaster as described on pages 94–95 and pour into the cottle. When dry, remove the vinyl and place the plaster shape onto the lathe.

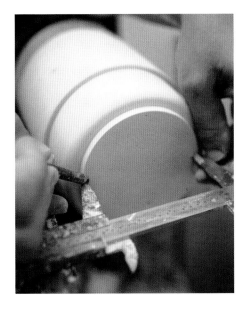 

3 Centring

Turn, using the chisel to smooth off rough sections and centre the plaster. Using the full-scale drawing, measure the finished diameter of the base with a pair of vernier callipers and mark a line on the plaster with a soft watercolour pencil that will not score the surface of the plaster.

4 Turning

Turn the model on the lathe, using the chisel to cut back the shape to your marked line. Keep referring back to the drawing at regular intervals for accurate modelling work. When the model is finished, use a fine wet and dry to smooth out the finished surface.

Making a drop-out mould

Soaping up

Try not to touch the model after you have soft-soaped it as the grease from your hands will almost certainly damage the waterproofing provided by the soft soap.

Remove the model and spare feed when the plaster is still warm, since it will be sweating slightly at this stage, which eases the process.

Earthenware slip will take around 15–20 minutes to cast to a suitable thickness. Porcelain slip will only take around 2–3 minutes. You may need to experiment to get the correct wall thickness for your project and the slip you are using.

1 Sealing the mould

Soak a plaster bat and spare feed in clean water so they are damp. Place the plaster bat, then the spare feed on a turntable, then add the model on the top. You can glue the separate layers temporarily together with a little craft glue so they don't move as you are working. Brush a layer of soft soap or mould-maker's size all over the model. Wipe the excess off with a damp sponge and clean water. Repeat this process three times to build up layers.

2 Releasing the model

Cottle around the whole model and plaster base as described on in step 2 on page 96. Mix the plaster as described on pages 94–95 and pour it into the vinyl cottle. Fill it up to around 2.5cm (1in) above the top of your model. As the plaster begins to set it will get quite warm and this is a good time to remove the plaster bat. Hold the whole mould off the work surface, place a metal weight on top and hit this sharply with a metal hammer to send a shock through the mould, releasing the model and the spare feed.

3 Pouring slip

Pour the slip into the drop out mould and leave to cast.

Making a two-part mould

Seaming well

The seamline needs to be at the widest point of the model all around, or the mould will have an undercut on one half that will make it difficult to release the finished slipcast piece.

When making the clay base in step 2, use a special modelling tool to take the clay as closely and neatly to the model along the seamline as possible, being very careful not to scratch the plaster model.

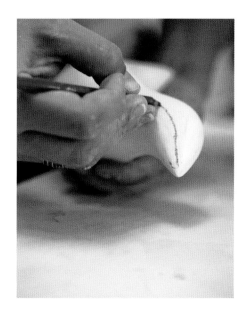

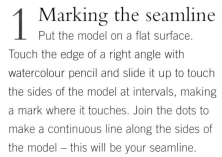

1 Marking the seamline
Put the model on a flat surface. Touch the edge of a right angle with watercolour pencil and slide it up to touch the sides of the model at intervals, making a mark where it touches. Join the dots to make a continuous line along the sides of the model – this will be your seamline.

2 Making the clay base
Soft soap the model as described in step 1 on page 98. Bury the whole model in clay, up to the level of the seamline all around the side. Cottle around the model and clay base and pour in plaster as described on page 95. Make sure you fill to 3cm (1¼in) above the top of the model.

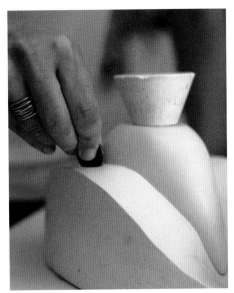

3 The pouring hole

When the plaster is dry remove the cottle and then remove all the clay. You now have the first half of the mould for the upper half of the bird. Place the model of the bird into the first half of the mould. On top of the model place the plaster bung to create a pouring hole and glue it in place.

4 Making the natches

Cut the natches or mould locators, by twisting a coin in a circular motion into the top edges of the finished half of the mould. Soft soap the whole thing three times, as described in step 1 on page 98. Finish by following step 2 on page 98. When the mould is dry it is ready for slipcasting.

Slipcasting

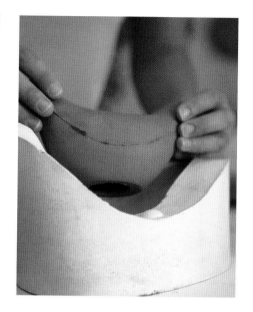

1 Pouring the slip

The mould should be fully dry, as dry plaster sucks water from the slip. Pour the slip continuously into the mould, going above the reservoir formed in the top. Leave the slip in the mould for the recommended time; the slip next to the plaster wall will begin to set.

2 Removing excess slip

Pour out the excess slip from the mould, then leave the mould upside down to drain and dry for at least half an hour. Cut and trim the excess clay from around the pouring hole.

3 Releasing the piece

Take the bands off the mould and carefully remove the top half. The clay will have shrunk slightly as it dries and moved away from the walls of the mould. The finished piece should come out quite easily. If it doesn't, leave it to dry out for a few more minutes.

Slipshape

Slip clay is normal clay with extra water and a chemical deflocculant that causes the particles of clay to remain suspended in the water rather than settling to the bottom.

Always sieve slip before using to remove larger particles. Stir gently to avoid introducing air bubbles.

Don't sponge the finished surface until the piece is completely dry, or the surface will look sponged rather than totally smooth.

Set a timer when pouring slip, as if left too long it can become too thick. About 15–20 minutes is about right to create a 4–5mm thick wall when using earthenware slip, but you may want to experiment to get the right thickness with other clay slips.

4 Smoothing seamlines

When the finished piece is dry, clean up the seamlines with a metal scraper or kidney. Leave to dry completely, then sponge to smooth off the surface.

Press moulding

Press ups

If you find a few small gaps in the
seamlines after you have removed the
finished form from the mould, you can
use small dabs of clay to fill them in.

Your press moulded form will be
hollow, so remember to place a small
hole somewhere out of sight to allow
the air to escape as it expands during
drying and firing.

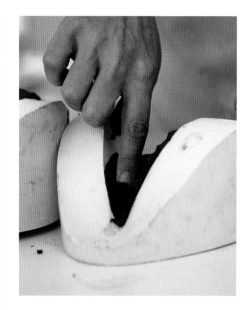

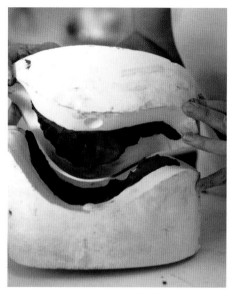

1 Pressing the clay
Use a two-part mould and press clay
into each half of the mould, going around
5mm (¼in) over the edges of the mould to
give you excess clay to join the halves
together. The walls should be around 5mm
(¼in) thick. You can also use slabs of clay
to press into the mould.

2 Joining the mould
When you have finished filling both
halves of the mould, press the two parts of
the mould together to join it – you may
need to apply quite a lot of weight and
pressure to force out the excess clay. Leave
for around 5 minutes for the clay to dry a
little in the plaster mould.

3 Cleaning seamlines

The seamlines will be quite ragged, so clean them up by scraping. Leave the piece to dry a little before smoothing further with the kidney and sponging.

intermediate
★★

small bowl

If you mention the word ceramics or pottery, one of the first objects people tend to think of is a bowl. Bowls can be functional or purely decorative, they have plenty of uses in the home or kitchen and can become treasured items. This project shows how to approach making a simple small pot for sugar, jam or snacks.

designer: Helen Johannessen

Materials

Plaster
Water
Bucket
String
Vinyl sheet
Soft soap
Brush
Plaster bat
Lathe
Vernier calliper
Watercolour pencil
Chisel
Earthenware clay slip
Metal weight
Hammer
Kidney tool
Sponge
Earthenware glaze

1 Draw up the design of your small bowl to the full size you will want to it be, then enlarge on the photocopier to allow for eventual shrinkage of the clay in the firing process – in this case 8–10% for earthenware slip.

2 Make a turned plaster model of your bowl, as described on pages 96–97, using your drawing as a guide.

3 Using the plaster model, make a drop-out mould as described on pages 98–99, and slipcast your bowl.

4 Pour the excess slip from the mould, then leave the bowl in the mould to dry.

5 Remove the bowl from the mould. The finished piece should come out quite easily. If it doesn't, leave it to dry for a few more minutes.

6 When the finished piece is dry, clean up the seamlines with a metal scraper or kidney and fettle with a sponge. Leave to dry completely.

7 Bisque fire the bowl to 1000–1060°C, as described on page 12.

8 To glaze the bowl see glazing techniques on pages 17–19. The glaze shown here was fired to 1140°C.

intermediate

★★

retro mugs

The simple household items that can be found in any home inspire many of my pieces. These mugs are given a wonderful retro look by the angular shape of handle, the starting point for which was the handle on a plastic jug I use in my studio. Don't be afraid to combine elements from different items to get the exact look that you want.

designer: Helen Johannessen

Materials

Spare clay for mould making
Plaster
Water
Bucket
String
Wood or plaster bats
Soft soap
Brush
Small coin
Metal weight
Hammer
Earthenware clay slip
Sieve
Jug
Kidney tool
Sponge
Earthenware glaze

1 Make a full size model of the body of your mug by turning it on the lathe as on pages 96–97, and place it on a flat surface. Model the handle from a block of plaster and stick to the body with glue in a place that suits. Follow the steps for a two-part mould on pages 100–101 to make your mould, but start by placing a spare feed or bung on top of the mug model to create the slipcasting pouring hole, and glue in place.

2 Lie the mug model on its side, pack it onto clay and make sure it is level. The seamline on this project will be straight as it runs through the centre of the handle and then straight across the bottom and up the other side of the mug. If you put a foot-ring into a mug like this, you would need a three-part mould to create the base.

3 Use plastic coated wood or soft soaped plaster bats for the walls to make this mould rectangular. Secure the walls with string as described in step 2 on page 96, before pouring the plaster. You can use extra clay to block any holes and further secure the walls.

4 Make sure you fill to at least 3cm (1¼in) above the top of the model. When the plaster is set remove the cottle and then remove all the clay. You now have the first half of the mould.

5 Cut the natches or mould locators, by twisting a coin in a circular motion into the top edges of the finished half of the mould. Soft soap the whole thing three times, as described in step 1 on page 98. Place and secure the walls around the side of the mould, as before. Pour the plaster. When the plaster has set and is becoming warm, use the weight and hammer to separate the mould and the feed from each other as described in step 2 on page 98. Once the mould has fully dried out, it is ready to use to slipcast.

6 Prepare the slip and cast your mug as described on pages 102–103.

7 When the finished piece is dry, fettle the seamlines with a metal scraper or kidney. Leave to dry completely, then sponge to smooth off the surface.

8 Bisque fire the mug to 1000°C, as described on page 12.

9 To glaze the mug see glazing techniques on pages 17–19; this particular glaze was fired to 1140°C.

intermediate
★ ★

face vase

The original inspiration for this vase was a book of portraits of chimps, with their appealing faces. I wanted to create a face on a vase, but portraying faces is very challenging and people react to them in different ways. The abstract shapes used here give the essential impression of a face – or may be regarded as merely a pleasing design.

designer: Tina Vlassopulos

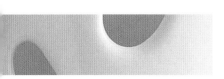

Materials

Plaster
Water
Bucket
String
Vinyl sheet
Soft soap
Brush
Plaster bat
Lathe
Callipers
Watercolour pencil
Chisel
Earthenware clay slip
Metal weight
Hammer
Kidney tool
Soft pencil
Potter's knife
Sponge or kitchen scourer
Earthenware glaze of your
   choice

See also

cutting out shapes in step 14
   on page 141.

1 Draw up the design of your vase to the full size.

2 Make a turned plaster model of your vase, as described on pages 96–97, using your drawing as a guide.

3 Using the plaster model, make a drop-out mould as described on pages 98–99, and slipcast your vase.

4 Pour the excess slip from the mould, then leave the vase in the mould to dry a little.

5 Remove the vase from the mould as described; the finished piece should come out quite easily. If it doesn't, leave it to dry for a few more minutes.

6 When the finished piece is leather hard, mark the shapes of the 'nose', 'eye' and 'mouth' with a soft pencil, then cut them out using a sharp potter's knife. Leave to dry completely, then sponge to smooth off the surface.

7 When the vase is bone dry, bisque fire it as described on page 12, following the instructions for the type of clay used.

8 To glaze the vase see glazing techniques on pages 17–19, then glaze fire according to the glaze manufacturer's instructions.

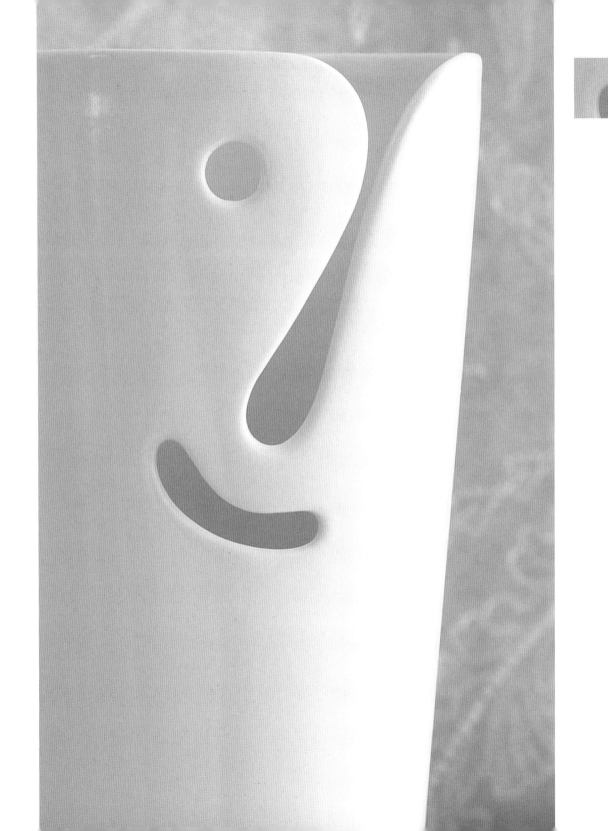

face vase 117

intermediate
★★

raku banana

It is easy to find inspirational objects to mould in your own home and it can be fun to use food, household items, or found objects. Plaster moulds are particularly good at mimicking texture – if you cast an orange, all the little dimples will come out. On this project the finish is raku, a traditional technique used for Japanese tea ceremony bowls.

designer: Helen Johannessen

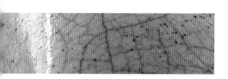

Materials

Banana
Spare clay for making mould
Plaster
Water
Bucket
String
Vinyl sheet
Soft soap
Brush
Right angle
Watercolour pencil
Modelling tool
Small coin
Metal weight
Hammer
Earthenware clay
Scraper
Kidney tool
Sponge
Props
Raku glaze
Tongs
Reduction chamber
Wood chips or straw

See also

raku firing on page 12.

1 The seamlines are quite obvious on a banana. This project was made with a press moulding technique, so start by making a two piece mould in the same way as the two piece mould described on pages 100–101, using your banana as a model and omitting the hole to feed the slip clay into.

2 Instead of pouring slip, press clay into each half of the mould as shown on pages 104–105, going around 5mm (¼in) over the edges of the mould to give you excess clay to join the halves of the form together. The walls should be around 5mm (¼in) thick.

3 When you have finished filling both halves of the mould, press the two parts of the mould together to join it – you may need to apply quite a lot of weight and pressure to force out the excess clay. Leave for around 5 minutes for the clay to dry a little in the plaster mould.

4 When removed from the mould, the seamlines on your banana will be quite ragged, so clean them up by scraping. If there are small gaps in the seamlines, use small dabs of clay to fill them. Leave the banana to dry a little before smoothing further with the kidney and sponging. The banana is hollow, so remember to place a small hole to allow the air to escape during drying and firing.

5 Bisque fire the banana to 1000°, as described on page 12.

6 Put the banana onto small props so that you can coat the entire form during the glazing process.

7 To glaze the banana, use Raku glaze and follow the instructions for pour glazing on page 17.

8 The raku technique (see page 12) involves removing the glazed banana from the kiln when the glaze is molten (around 900ºC), using tongs. The glazed banana is then put in an airtight reduction chamber and covered with wood chips or straw, which gives the typical black crackle.

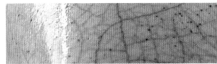

Press gang

Press moulding is a good technique for people who want to use moulds but don't have the facilities to do slipcasting. You can also alter and add to the shape you have pressed as the clay you use is more malleable than slipcasting clay generally.

Raku pieces are often not very watertight, so should be regarded as decorative not functional.

intermediate
★ ★

lace lights

This is a fantastic way to create delicate ambient lighting for your home using basic mould making skills. Light up your interior with these pretty little pieces of ceramic, inspired by intricate antique lace from the 1800s.

designer: Charlie Atkin

Materials

Clay for modelling
Plastic sheet
Rolling pin
Roller guides
Lace or textured wallpaper
Potter's knife or scalpel
Cookie cutter about 9cm
  (3½ in) in diameter
Circular former (optional)
Plaster
Water
Bucket
String
Vinyl sheet
Soft soap
Brush
Plaster bat, Lathe
Vernier calliper
Watercolour pencil
Chisel
Bone china clay slip
Metal weight
Hammer, Kidney tool
Sponge, Clear glaze

See also

slabbing steps 1–4 on pages
  44–45
joining shapes on page 25.

1 Prepare your clay slab as described on in steps 1–3 on pages 44–45. Roll it no thicker than 5mm (¼in) although remember it will roll thinner when textured.

2 Lay the lace or wallpaper over the cut section of slab with the roller guides still in place and roll again to impress the design into the clay.

3 Cut a section of slab 8 x 20cm (3¼ x 8in) for the body of the light. Use the cookie cutter to cut the base. Remember to make your model larger as the size will shrink when the clay is fired; bone china will shrink by approx 14%.

4 Using a scalpel or knife score one long edge and the two short edges in a cross hatching fashion as well as the outermost 5mm (¼in) of the round piece of slab. Be careful not to actually slice into the clay. The aim is to go no deeper than a millimetre.

5 Apply slip to the scored short edges using a small paintbrush and join carefully. If necessary use a cardboard roll or piece of plastic pipe of the right thickness to form around – first tape a double layer of newspaper loosely around it so the clay slips off easily after forming. Push the scored edges together firmly but gently until the slip begins to ooze out. Use your finger or a modelling tool to seal the join and smooth it down on both sides of the join. Make sure you support the opposite side of the join at all times.

6 Leave the model of the light to dry until it is leather hard, then cast it in plaster to make a drop-out mould as described on pages 98–99.

7 Use the drop-out mould to slipcast the lights, following the instructions on pages 102–103.

8 Pour the excess slip from the mould, and then leave the bowl in the mould to dry until the shine has completely gone from the slip. While still in the mould create a small tear at the rim of the vessel and roll your finger around the edge to create the torn edge. You may have to practice this a few times to get the right effect.

9 Remove the bowl from the mould. The finished piece should come out quite easily. If it doesn't, leave it to dry for a while longer.

10 Bisque fire the bowl to 1260°C, as described on page 12.

11 To glaze the bowl, see glazing techniques on pages 17–19. The glaze shown here was fired to 1080–1100°C.

advanced techniques

This section has rather more advanced projects, that build on the techniques learned in earlier chapters but take them that little bit further. The Distorted Vase begins with throwing, but then the resulting shape is reformed. The Bird uses a waste mould technique, and is decorated with cut-outs, while transfers are used in the following project. And finally, the teapot illustrates the techniques for making a spout and a lid.

advanced
★★★

distorted vase

This thrown and altered porcelain vase was initially inspired by folding paper. I start from the basic process of wheel throwing, then a process of altering, cutting, folding and assembling the clay allows my curiosity to explore and play with the plasticity of the material and also to investigate my own sense of beauty.

designer: Sun Kim

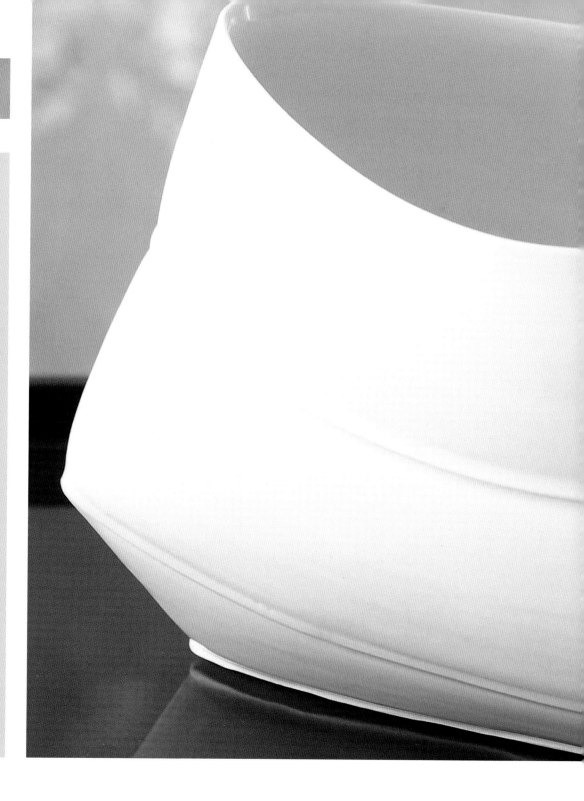

Materials

Porcelain clay
Bat
Wheel
Water
Sponge
Rib tool
Sharp cutting tool
Glaze of your choice

1 Prepare 2kg (4lb 6oz) of clay as described on page 68. To throw the basic shape begin by following the throwing steps 2–5 on pages 68–69, but keep pressing down towards the base of your clay until you have created a ring of clay with an empty centre.

2 With your left hand fingers inside the ring and your thumb gripping the outside wall, begin lifting the wall of a cylinder by pressing the clay from both sides, while keeping the wheel moving.

3 The final shape of the cylinder is formed and smoothed by using a throwing rib. Start just above the base and use the rib on the outside wall, supporting the inside with your thumb. The final stages of shaping should be made with the wheel moving very slowly.

distorted vase 131

  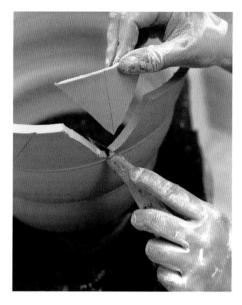

4 Use the rib tool to shape three
   sections each of an equal size on the
sides of the cylinder.

5 Remove the cylinder from the bat as
   described in step 8 on page 70, let it
dry for couple of hours and turn it over.

6 Cut four triangular sections out of the
   rim, two on each opposite side of the
cylinder, cutting down to the bottom of the
first section.

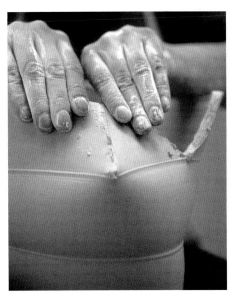

7 Gently push in on the sides of the cylinder to alter it into an oval shape, with the cut out triangular sections placed at each end.

8 Score the edges of the cut out sections and apply clay slip for joining. Fold the edges inwards so they join and smooth the join. Turn the body back over again.

9 Roll out a slab of flat clay and attach it to the bottom of the pot. Cut around the base, making the shape of the bottom piece slightly bigger.

10 Turn the pot over and trim the edges of the bottom to the sides of the pot. Allow the pot to completely dry.

11 Bisque fire the bowl to 1000°C, as described on page 12.

12 To glaze the bowl see glazing techniques on pages 17–19, then glaze fire following the recommendations for your chosen glaze.

advanced
★★★

bird

It can be satisfying to sculpt in clay as the material lends itself to organic forms that can morph into shape as you work. It is often hard to make really smooth and fluid surfaces directly in clay, but this waste mould technique shows how you can achieve very crisp detail. The bird form was chosen for it simple shape and size.

designer: Helen Johannessen

Materials

Spare clay for model making
Plaster bats
Soft soap
Brush
Vinyl sheet
String
Plaster
Water
Bucket
Saw
Splitting tool
Hammer
Earthenware casting slip
Sieve
Jug
Kidney tool

Small cutter
Sponge
Earthenware glaze

See also

making a two-part mould on
   pages 100–101
slipcasting on pages
   102–103.

1 Make your solid clay model, smoothing the surface with your fingers as much as you can.

2 Soft soap a small bat a few times to build up the layers, then set up your model in the centre making sure there is around 3cm (1¼in) space all around to the edge of the bat to allow for the thickness of the mould wall. Cottle around the edge of the bat as described in step 2 on page 96.

3 Mix the plaster as described on pages 94–95 and pour it into the vinyl cottle, covering the model to about 2.5cm (1in) above the top. Leave the plaster to set.

Supermodel

The initial model does not have to be solid, but you don't have to make it hollow either.

Working over the surface of the model with fine wet and dry gives a smooth, polished look to the finished surface.

There are lots of special tools you can buy for working with clay and plaster, but don't be afraid to use anything from around the house or kitchen that you think will be suitable. For instance, old credit cards are good as scrapers, old butter knives are good for shaping, plastic kitchen utensils can be cut down.

4 Score all around the sides of the mould with a saw roughly along the centre line.

5 Remove the bat that was used as the base to reveal the bottom of your clay model showing on one side of the waste mould. Use a splitting tool and a hammer along the scored line. Work around the mould at intervals to split it into pieces.

6 Don't worry too much about how many pieces the plaster finally breaks into, as this is only a waste mould. Remove the clay model from the mould. Soft soap all the inside surfaces of the mould.

7 The hole in the base of your waste mould, where the clay model touched the bat, will form the pouring hole. Place the pieces of the mould back together and glue in place.

8 Use some string to hold the pieces of the mould firmly together. Pour plaster into the waste mould through the base hole to fill up the entire mould interior.

9 Leave to dry, then pull the waste mould apart and remove the solid plaster cast model. You may need to use a weight and hammer to tap the mould to ease removal of the plaster.

10 Use a surform, files, rasps and scrapers to sculpt the shape, then use the finest grade wet and dry to smooth the surfaces of the model.

11 Use the model you have made to make a two-part mould, as described on pages 100–101.

12 Sieve the slip into a jug to remove any lumps. Slipcast your bird as described on pages 102–103.

 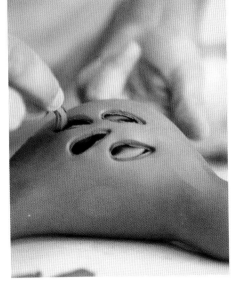

13 When the finished piece is dry, fettle the seam lines with a metal scraper or kidney. Leave to dry completely, then sponge to smooth off the surface.

14 When the bird is leather hard, add the cut out decoration. Use small shaped cutters to cut out a decorative design on the sides, being careful to cut neatly and not distort the shape.

15 Bisque fire the bird to 1000°C, as described on page 12.

16 To glaze the bird see glazing techniques on pages 17–19; this particular clear glaze was fired to 1140°C.

advanced
★★★

picture perfect

Transfer (or decal) work produces quite a unique
decorative result. The transfers are applied onto glazed
ware as a final touch and can produce sharp and bright
colours or images. Traditionally, the transfer sheets were
silkscreened (and still are) but the digital age means
they can now also be computer generated, and
produced using special printers.

designer: Helen Johannessen

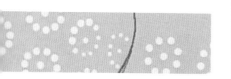

Materials

Finished clay form, already
  glazed
Transfers
Sharp scissors
Water
Rubber kidney

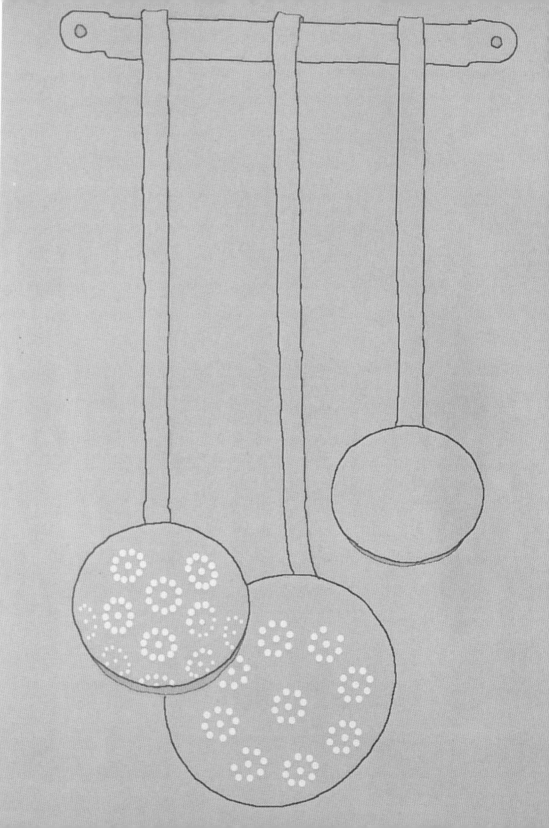

 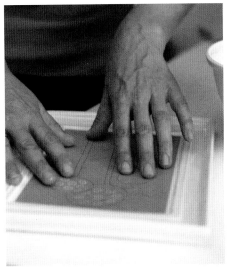 

1 Transfers are special enamel ink printed or screened onto a special paper, with a cover coat applied on top to hold the colours, which can be fired onto a glazed surface. Cut out the motif you want to transfer and place it into warm water to soften and remove the backing paper. This leaves you with the cover coat and colours ready to apply onto your piece.

2 Place the transfer onto the glazed ceramic. Since it is still wet you can slide it around to position it carefully.

3 Very carefully and working from the inside out, smooth a rubber kidney across the transfer to remove any excess water and air bubbles. If there is any water left under the transfer it will lift off when the model is fired, and air bubbles will lead to missing sections of the design as it will tend to 'burn out'.

4 When the transfers are all in place and dry, position the items in the kiln with space in between them and fire at around 800°C – check the supplier's recommendation, as firing temperatures will vary. The glaze will soften slightly at the top temperature, allowing the transfer to fuse into the glazed surface permanently.

Design notes

Leave the transfer to dry thoroughly before you put the item into the kiln – this will allow the design to set more evenly.

When putting transfers onto curved surfaces, soak them in warm water so they will stretch slightly around the curves.

Digitally produced transfers are printed using ceramic oxide inks. Although the quality can be less sharp than screened ones, the digital types can be more flexible in design.

advanced
★★★

spring green
teapot

Taking tea is an ancient tradition and to me it signifies
a group of people gathering together in a social
atmosphere. I love the sense of ceremony that using
a teapot brings to the occasion – it is more formal than
just making tea in a mug. The inspiration for the curving
shape of this teapot comes from the traditional pots
found in Japan.

designer: Katie Adams

Materials

Stoneware clay
Wheel
Water
Kidney tool
Turning tool
Sponge
Cutting wire
Glaze of your choice

See also

throwing steps 2–7 and
    step 10 on pages 68–71.

Out of your depth

When turning the lid, remember to leave a good depth of clay underneath so you have a thickness of clay to turn the knob into later.

Bisque fire and glaze fire the teapot and lid at the same time, so they will shrink at the same rate – otherwise they may not fit together well when the teapot is finished.

1 Start by wedging the clay by kneading it thoroughly to remove any air bubbles, as described on page 8. Weigh out 1588g (3½lb) of clay for the teapot, 113g (¼lb) for the spout and 113g (¼lb) for the lid.

2 Throw the body of the teapot as described in the basic throwing steps 2–7 on pages 68–70. As you lift the wall, with your left hand turn your wrist so the pads of the three fingers on the inside and the supporting thumb on the outside create the curve of the sides.

3 To throw the galley in the pot, support the rim on the outside with your thumb and press down inside with your index finger to create a curving ledge.

4 The following day, turn the pot over and carve the foot ring into the base as described in step 10 on page 71.

5 The lid is thrown upside down to start. Centre the clay, open a pot shape up in the middle, but leave a wide rim. Holding the inner wall steady with your middle finger, pull the clay up underneath with your thumb and at the same time flatten out on top with the index finger. Measure the width of the lid with callipers to make sure it will fit your pot. Leave a depth of clay underneath to turn the knob into later.

6 To form the lip in the inner wall of the lid, support the outside of the wall with your thumb and index finger. With the index finger of the other hand, bend the wall out and shape it into a lip. Leave to dry until leather hard.

7 Turn the lid over. Sponge the wheel head and rim of lid, centre the lid and tap it to attach. With the wheel head turning at medium speed, use the turning tool to shape the knob – it can be as wide as you want it.

8 Measure the width of the lid with callipers again to make sure that it will still fit your pot. With a tapered hole cutter, carefully bore a hole in the lid so the steam can escape.

9 Throw the spout in a small bottle shape in proportion to the teapot. Leave it to dry until it is leather hard. Cut an angle of around 60° off the bottom of the spout, then shape it so that it fits snugly to the curved side of the teapot.

10 Draw around the base of the spout with a blade to mark where it will fit on the teapot. Score the base of the spout and wet the score lines with water.

11 Score the body of the teapot where you have marked the position of the spout and again wet with water.

12 With the tapered hole cuter, cut holes into the body of the pot within the spout area.

 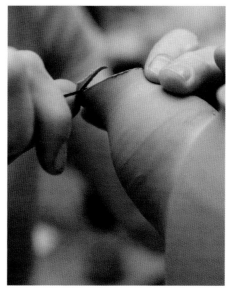 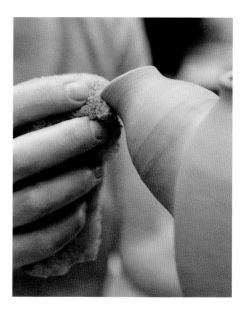

13 Attach the spout to the body of the teapot and feed a fine coil of clay right around the join to strengthen it. Smooth the join first with your fingers and then with a sponge.

14 Trim an angle off the top of the spout so that it is level with the rim of the teapot.

15 Smooth round the edges of the rim of the spout with a sponge.

 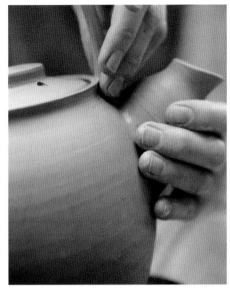

16 From a firm lump of clay, with wet hands pull down evenly to extend the clay down into a handle. It is very important to pull in long even strokes. Flatten the length back and front so the handle is flat not circular, creating a thick ribbon of clay. Curve the handle round into roughly the shape you want and leave it to dry until it is leather hard. This will not take long as it is quite small.

17 Pick up the handle and place it on top of the pot. Mark where the ends join the pot, score the ends of the handle and the pot and add water at the score lines. Press the handle ends onto the pot and work in so it is firmly and smoothly attached.

18 Leave the teapot and lid to dry thoroughly, which will take at least 24 hours.

19 Bisque fire both the teapot and the lid together so they will shrink at the same rate and keep their fit to one another, firing to 1000°C as described on page 12.

20 To glaze the teapot and lid see glazing techniques on pages 17–19, then glaze fire to 1260°C or follow the recommended instructions for your chosen glaze.

Glossary

bat – a flat plaster or wooden disk used as a base when throwing or moving pots around.

batch – a mixture of weighed materials such as a batch of glaze or slip or a clay body.

banding wheel – A turntable on a pedestal base that is turned by hand and used for finishing or decorating pottery.

bisque – clay items after the first firing without glaze, usually at around 1000°C (1832°F).

bone dry – completely air-dried.

burnishing – a rubbing process to polish the outside skin of a leather hard clay item, to smooth, compact the surface and reduce porosity. It is done by hand, using a stone or a metal piece.

casting – making items by pouring liquid clay slip into plaster moulds.

ceramic – item made in some kind of clay that has been fired in a kiln.

centring – moving the clay in to a symmetrical rotating axis in the middle of a wheel head so you can throw it.

china clay – a non-plastic clay body that is usually mixed with other clays.

chuck – a form to hold a pot upside-down above the wheel head while it is trimmed. Chucks are thrown and bisque-fired clay cylinders open on both sides.

coiling – forming an item from coiling round ropes of clay.

composite pots – pots thrown or hand built in separate pieces and then assembled.

cottle – wall around a shape that is to be cast in plaster.

crazing – fine cracks caused by glaze shrinking on the surface at a different rate to the clay form. Also known as crackling.

deflocculant – chemical that causes the particles of clay in slip to remain in suspension.

dipping – immersing an object to apply slip or glaze.

earthenware – the most common and least expensive clay with a low firing temperature or pottery fired at a low temperature. It is porous, so must be glazed to make it watertight.

fettle – turning and cleaning up dry or bisque fired pots.

firing – heating clay items in a kiln to harden or to glaze.

flange – rim around the inside of a lid and the matching ledge around the inside of the top of a pot, which is used to locate and support the lid. Also called a gallery.

foot – base on which a piece of pottery stands.

foot ring – a rim turned into the base of a pot so that it will stand flat and evenly.

gallery – see flange.

glaze – thin vitreous layer that is applied to clay items and then fired to fuse it to the surface. It can be used both to waterproof and to decorate.

glaze firing – the final firing, with glaze applied.

gloss glaze – a shiny reflective gloss finish.

greenware – unfired pottery ready to be bisque fired.

incise – cutting a line or design of some kind into the surface with a sharp point.

kidney tool – a scraper made of plastic, wood or rubber.

kneading – rolling and pressing the clay to disperse moisture evenly and prepare it for use.

leather hard – the stage of the clay between wet and bone dry. Clay is still damp enough to join it to other pieces using slip. For example, this is the stage handles are applied to mugs.

majolica – a low fire glazing technique. The process involves applying an opaque tin glaze to earthenware and painting it with different coloured oxides.

matt glaze – a dull glaze surface, not very reflective when fired. It needs a slow cooling period or it may turn shiny.

mould – a hollow plaster shape in which to pour clay slip, so that it will dry into an exact replica of the model used to make the mould.

opaque glaze – a non-transparent glaze that will cover the clay or glaze below it.

oxidation – firing with a full supply of oxygen to achieve bright colours.

pinching – manipulating clay with your fingers to make a hollow shape.

plastic – a quality of clay that allows it to be manipulated into different shapes without cracking or breaking, and to stay in shape.

porcelain – white translucent clay, made from feldspar, china clay, flint and whiting, which can be fired at up to 1300ºC (2372ºF) and can give very translucent items.

potters' plaster – a type of plaster that is mixed with water and hardens in a chemical process. Also sometimes called plaster of paris.

potters' wheel – a rotating wheel head powered by a foot pedal or an electric rotating motor that is used to make pottery forms.

press moulding – pressing slabs of clay over items or moulds to form a shape.

raku – a form of firing that was traditionally used in Japan, in which the items are fired to a high temperature very quickly and taken out of the kiln still hot, while the glaze is liquid. They are then plunged into a drum of wood chips, sawdust or straw, which is sealed. The rapid cooling causes the glaze to crackle, allowing the smoke from the burning sawdust or straw to penetrate the surface.

resist – wax, latex or paper used to prevent glaze fusing to an area of the clay, creating a decorative effect.

rib – a wooden or plastic tool used to raise the sides of a pot when throwing.

satin glaze – a glaze between matt and gloss.

slab – pressed or rolled flat sections of clay.

slip – clay mixed with water to the consistency of double cream and used for casting and decoration.

slurry – very liquid clay, created when hard pieces of unfired clay are left to soak in warm water to reclaim dried-out clay for further use.

soak – the process of leaving the kiln at the recommended maturation temperature for a short period before shutting it down to cool.

soft soap – semi-liquid soap that is used as a release agent when casting with moulds.

sponging – applying slip or glaze with a sponge, or cleaning and smoothing the surface of pottery before firing.

stamping – using a stamp or found object to press a design into a clay surface.

stoneware – clays that are denser and harder than earthenware, which are made into ceramic items fired at high temperatures of between 1200–1300ºC (2192–2372ºF).

terracotta – earthenware clay with a high iron content that fires to a deep red-brown.

transparent glaze – a clear glaze that shows the clay or the underglaze colour beneath.

throwing – creating ceramic shapes on the potter's wheel.

underglaze – colour applied to greenware or bisque-fired pottery and usually then covered with transparent glaze.

vitrification – firing of pottery to the point that the clay particles fuse together and become vitreous. This makes the item impervious to liquids.

wedging – method of mixing clay by cutting and pressing, either to mix different clays together or to make it even and air-free ready for use.

wet clay – clay that is still plastic and ready to work

Designers

KATIE ADAMS
Studio W3
Cockpit Arts
Northington Street
London WC1N 2NP
Web: www.katieadamsceramics.com
Email:bodypot@gmail.com

CHARLIE ATKIN
3 Glyn Morlas
St Martins
Oswestry
Shropshire SY11 3EE
Email:charlie.atkin@btopenworld.com

LIZ EMTAGE
Studio E15
Cockpit Arts
Northington Street
London WC1N 2NP
Web: www.lizemtageceramics.com
Email: liz@lizemtageceramics.com

ALEX HAGEN
Studio 2E–D
Vanguard Court
36–38 Peckham Road
London SE5 8QT
Email: alexhagen@btinternet.com

JO HECKETT
Studio E16
Cockpit Arts
Northington Street
London WC1N 2NP
Web: www.joheckett.com
Email: jo@joheckett.com

HELEN JOHANNESSEN
Yoyo Ceramics
Studio E16
Cockpit Arts
Northington Street
London WC1N 2NP
Web: www.yoyoceramics.co.uk
Email: helen@yoyoceramics.co.uk

CHRIS KEENAN
Studio 7C
Vanguard Court
36–38 Peckham Road
London SE5 8QT
Web: www.chriskeenan.com
Email: chris@chriskeenan.com

SUN KIM
Studio 2E–D
Vanguard Court
36–38 Peckham Road
London SE5 8QT
Email: sunkim_77@yahoo.com

MERETE RASMUSSEN
Studio 2E–D
Vanguard Court
36–38 Peckham Road
London SE5 8QT
Web: www.mereterasmussen.com
Email: mr@mereterasmussen.com

TINA VLASSOPULOS
29 Canfield Gardens
London NW6 3JP
Web: www.tinavlassopulos.com
Email: tina@tinavlassopulos.com

UK Resources

Bath Potters' Supplies
Unit 18 Fourth Avenue
Westfield Trading Estate
Radstock
Bath BA3 4XE
Tel: 01761 411077
Email: sales@bathpotters.co.uk
www.bathpotters.co.uk
Clays, glazes, equipment, kiln accessories, tools.

Ceramatech Limited
Units 16&17 Frontier Works
33 Queen Street
Tottenham North
London N17 8JA.
Tel: 0208 885 4492
Email: info@ceramatech.co.uk
www.ceramatech.co.uk
Clays, glazes, equipment, kiln accessories, tools.

Country Love Ceramics
Unit 37d
Milton Park
Abingdon OX14 4RT
www.countryloveceramics.com
Kilns, bisque, paint and more.

CTM Supplies
Unit 1b Millpark Industrial Estate
White Cross Road
Woodbury Salterton EX5 1EL
Tel: 01395 233077
Email: ctmsupplies@hemscott.net
www.ctmsupplies.co.uk
Tools, glazes.

Digital Ceramics
Quantum House
290 Leek Road
Stoke-on-Trent
Staffordshire ST4 2EJ
Tel: 01782 215400
info@digitalceramics.com
www.digitalceramics.com
Transfers.

Hobby Ceramicraft
www.hobbyceramicraft.co.uk
Clays, glazes, equipment, kiln accessories, tools.

Potclays Limited
Brickkiln Lane,
Etruria
Stoke-on-Trent,
Staffordshire, ST4 7BP
Tel: 01782 219816
Email: sales@potclays.co.uk
www.potclays.co.uk
Clays, glazes, equipment, kiln accessories, tools.

Potterycraft
Campbell Road
Stoke-on-Trent ST4 4ET
Tel: 01782 745000
Email: enquiries@potterycrafts.co.uk
www.potterycrafts.co.uk
Clays, glazes, equipment, kiln accessories, tools.

Scarva Pottery Supplies
Unit 20 Scarva Road Industrial Estate
Scarva Road
County Down BT32 3QD
Tel: 028 40669699
Email: david@scarvapottery.com
www.scarvapottery.com
Equipment, kiln accessories, tools.

Travis Perkins
Branches nationwide
Tel: 01604 752424
www.travisperkins.co.uk
Plaster.

US Resources

A.R.T Studito Clay Company
9320 Michigan Ave.
Sturtevant, WI 53177-2425
Tel: 877-ART-CLAY
www.artclay.com
*Glazes, clays, tools, wheels and kiln
equipment.*

Axner Pottery Supply
490 Kane Ct.
Oviedo, FL 32765
Tel: 800-843-7057 or 407-365-2600
www.axner.com
*Clays, glazes, equipment, kiln
accessories, tools.*

Ceramic Supply, Inc.
7 Route 46 West
Lodi, NJ 07644
Tel: 800-723-7264
Email: orders@eceramicsupply.com
www.7ceramic.com
*Clays, glazes, equipment, kiln
accessories, tools.*

Charles B. Chrystal Co, Inc.
30 Vesey Street
New York, NY 10007
Tel: 212-227-2151

Email: info@cbchrystal.com
www.cbchrystal.com
Clays, plaster.

Clayworks Supplies, Inc.
4625 Falls Rd.
Baltimore, MD 21209
Tel: 410-235-5998
www.clayworkssupplies.com
*Clays, glazes, tools, equipment, and
books.*

**Highwater Clays Ceramic Supplies &
Equipment**
600 Riverside Dr.
Asheville, NC 28801
Tel: 828-252-6033
www.highwaterclays.com
*Clays, ceramic supplies, and
equipment.*

Tucker's Pottery Supplies, Inc.
15 W. Pearce St.
Richmond Hill, ONT L4B 1H6
Canada
Tel: 800-304-6185
www.tuckerspottery.com
*Books, stains, clays, decorating and
finishing supplies, glazes, and more.*

Index

ACKNOWLEDGEMENTS

With thanks to Katie Adams, Charlie Atkin, Liz Emtage, Alex Hagen,
Jo Heckett, Helen Johannessen, Chris Keenan, Sun Kim,
Merete Rasmussen and Tina Vlassopulos.
With special thanks to Marie Clayton for editing the book and Jaqui Atkin for
her expertise and advice.

PICTURE CREDITS

Project photography by Holly Jolliffe.
Step-by-step photography by Mark Winwood.
Photography on page 16 left, and pages 42, 44–45, 55–57, 123–125
by Dan Duchars.